YoungWri
POETRY COMP

GREAT MINDS

Your World...Your Future...YOUR WORDS

From Shropshire
Edited by Jessica Woodbridge

Young Writers

First published in Great Britain in 2005 by:
Young Writers
Remus House
Coltsfoot Drive
Peterborough
PE2 9JX
Telephone: 01733 890066
Website: www.youngwriters.co.uk

All Rights Reserved

© *Copyright Contributors 2004*

SB ISBN 1 84460 693 7

Foreword

This year, the Young Writers' 'Great Minds' competition proudly presents a showcase of the best poetic talent selected from over 40,000 up-and-coming writers nationwide.

Young Writers was established in 1991 to promote the reading and writing of poetry within schools and to the youth of today. Our books nurture and inspire confidence in the ability of young writers and provide a snapshot of poems written in schools and at home by budding poets of the future.

The thought, effort, imagination and hard work put into each poem impressed us all and the task of selecting poems was a difficult but nevertheless enjoyable experience.

We hope you are as pleased as we are with the final selection and that you and your family continue to be entertained with *Great Minds From Shropshire* for many years to come.

Contents

Abraham Darby School
Danielle Groves (12)	1
Shane Payne (12)	1
Chris Pettitt (12)	2
Stewart Boffey (12)	2
Danielle Spencer (12)	3
Charlotte Elvin (11)	3
Sarah Smith (12)	4
Hannah Griffiths (12)	5
Natalie Edwards (12)	6
Daniel Onions (12)	6
Faye Edwards & Jamie Smith (15)	7
Patrick Matthews (12)	7
Sophie Olver (13)	8
Sudeep Singh (12)	8
Kerry Clarke (11)	9
Amy Trewartha (12)	9
Rebecca Powell (12)	10
Shaun Coldicutt (11)	10
James Pilling (11)	11
Zahid Reza (12)	11
Thomas Managh (11)	12
Nathan Moore (11)	12
Lauren Price (11)	13
Candice Smith (11)	14
Parês Thomas (11)	14
Robert Wenlock (11)	15
Matthew Burrows (12)	15
Chelsea Lowe (11)	16
Tammy Muddell (12)	16
Siân Smith (12)	17
Carla Rann (12)	17
Kirsty Colclough (11)	18
Scott Brough (14)	18
Katie O'Hanlon (12)	18
Tara Atterbury (12)	19
Daniel Heaword (12)	19
Hayley Watton (12)	19
Danny Perkins (12)	20

Christopher Baxter (12)   20
Luke Underwood (13)   21
Oliver Yardley (12)   21
Alex Bridgwater (12)   22
Natalie Resoun (13)   22
James Powis (12)   22
Jayne Collis (12)   23
Katherine Evans (12)   23
Charlotte Wade (12)   23
Damien Griffiths (12)   24
Oliver Rimmer (12)   24
Jonathan Webster (12)   24
Alexander Durnall (11)   25
Liam Baldi (13)   25
Chris Trafford (12)   25
Eleanor Ballinger (11)   26
Alex Fallon (13)   27

Meole Brace School
Bethany Gentempo (12)   27
Joseph Ruxton (13)   28
Neil Love (13)   28
Lucia James (13)   29
Jenny Collins (13)   30
Liam Shaw (13)   30
Sam Kenney (12)   31
Quentin Otto (13)   31
Megan Williams (12)   32
Danny Williams (15)   32
Tim Farrow (11)   33
Shannon Mosley (13)   33
Jade Colley (12)   34
Rebecca Lawn (13)   34
Bryony Smith (12)   35
Paddy Anderson Loake (11)   35
Emily Marston (13)   36
Laura Causey (12)   37
Dom Sadd (12)   38
Will Heath (12)   39
Kelli Swancott (13)   40
Nick Jones (11)   40

Sammy Morris (14)	41
Jonathan Bunce (12)	41
Sarah Chambers (13)	42
Jazmin Highfield (11)	42
Nick Stephens (13)	43
Amy Price (13)	43
Will Jones (13)	44
Hannah Morgan (13)	45
Hannah Swallow (13)	46
Rebecca Wallen (13)	47
Matthew Jones (13)	48
Andy Bullough (13)	48
Robert Cannell (12)	49
Emily Robinson (11)	49
Ashley Titley (12)	50
Chris Evans (12)	51
Lucy Buzzacott (13)	52
Andrew Jones (12)	53
Laura Roberts (12)	54
Kirsten Jones (13)	55
Tom Burke (13)	56
James Robinson (13)	57
Will Andrews (13)	58
Toby Kirk (14)	59
Ricky Evans (13)	60
Molly Derbyshire (11)	60
Peter Kilby (13)	61
Annabelle Bowyer (13)	61
Alex Roberts (13)	62
Douglas Tenison-Collins (11)	62
Lucy Baker (14)	63
Rachel Austin (11)	63
Harriet Cockill (14)	64
Alice Windows (13)	65
Laura Gwilliams (14)	66
Elliot Townsend (11)	66
Rebecca Ellis (14)	67
Ruth Lunt (11)	67
Natalie Robson (11)	68
Robert Carey (11)	68
Robert Clayton (13)	69
Jessica Marsden (11)	69

Amy Lewis (11)	70
Lauren Gwilt (12)	70
Kathryn Donnelly (11)	71
Phoebe Ruxton (12)	71
Anthony Smith (13)	72
Hazel Tetsill (12)	72
Vicky Taylor (13)	73
Stephen Barnard (12)	73
Michael L'argent (13)	74
James Carter (11)	74
Jamie Holden (12)	75
Alice Bowen (13)	75
Anneka Gorman (14)	76
Matt Clough (13)	76
Sian O'Hanlon (13)	77
Sebastian Salamat (12)	77
Ellen Brenner (12)	78
Becky Lloyd (13)	78
Bassam Khalaileh (12)	79
Josh Meredith (13)	79
Alex Cartwright (12)	80
Melissa Thorpe (13)	80
Jessica Gale (12)	81
Daniel Morris (13)	81
Pippa Cox (13)	82
Dannielle Natasha Tennant (13)	82
Kate Brett (12)	83
Hannah Mainwaring (12)	83
Gemma Cusack (13)	84
Sam Whittaker (12)	84
Ebony May Pharo (13)	85
Caldy Walton (12)	85
Ellen Alexander (11)	86
Danielle Haywood (13)	86
Charlotte Lewis (11)	87
Annie Lam (12)	87
Robert Wilson (13)	88
Susannah Williams (12)	88
Robert Edward Howarth Savage (12)	88
Harriet Davies (12)	89
Callum Chatham (12)	89
Michael Abbott (12)	89

Brad Smith (11)	90
Callum Bebb (12)	90
Aidan Lo (12)	90
Amy Lewis (12)	91
Chris Duffy (12)	91
Hayley Jenks (12)	92
Joe Streeter (12)	92
Connor Marston (12)	93
Roseanna Corsentino (11)	93
Jessica Mullineaux (11)	94
Rachael Thomas (13)	94
David Payne (12)	95
Jessica Beardmore (13)	95
Millie Goodman (11)	96
Amy Fletcher (11)	96
Aidan Wilkes (11)	97
Lucy Shaddock (13)	97
Sarah Lawrence (13)	98
Tineka Frost (11)	99
Francesca Huffa (12)	100
Chris Sturge (13)	100
Sam Noakes (11)	101
Natalia Kirby (12)	101
Charlotte Jones (11)	102
Jean Hughes (11)	102
Kris Jackson (11)	103
Lily Cribbin (13)	103
Poppy Olah (13)	104
James Bruce (12)	104
Nicola Thomas (11)	105
Matthew Hemstock (12)	105
Francine Hartshorn (13)	106
Jacob Tiernan (11)	106
Claire Jones (13)	107
Natasha Hall (13)	108
Anna Davies (13)	109
Rosie Marsh (13)	110
Jenny Hosty (12)	110
Husnain Shah (12)	111
Oliver Edwards (12)	111
Jessica Parry (13)	112
Nik Edwards (11)	112

Rioja Gwynne-Porter (12) 113
Louise Jones (12) 113
Nathan Hinks (11) 114
Katie Davies (13) 114
Joseph Shaw (12) 115
Jacob Olah (11) 115
Matt Galliers (13) 116
Matthew Dodd (11) 116
Joseph Kenneth Lunt (12) 117
Scott Bentley (11) 117
Sasha Rocke (13) 118
Rianna Matthews (11) 118
Jack Tomkiss (11) 119
Anna Bevan (13) 119
Ash Keville (11) 120
Charlotte Davies (11) 120
Tom Swallow (11) 121
Natalie Fisher (13) 121
Rob Jones (12) 122
Eleanor Smith (13) 122
Lucy Cockill (11) 123
Luke Edge (13) 123
Rebecca Dowley (12) 124
Lyle Sambrook (11) 124
Anouzka Lowrie-Herz (11) 124
Jessica Gough (13) 125
Chris Ferris (12) 125
Vicky Roberts (12) 125
Luca Furio (12) 126
John Goodall (13) 126
Lucas Taylor (12) 126
Sian Owen (11) 127
Polly-Anna Lloyd (12) 127

Moreton Hall School
Grace Meehan (12) 128
Katie Christy (12) 128
Katie Stearns (12) 129
Ebony Ewington (11) 129
Philippa Woodside (12) 130
Laura Davies (12) 130

Charlotte Rose Doel (12)	131
Jennifer Davies (12)	131
Lucy Emberton (12)	132
Chloe England (11)	132
Jemma Moore (12)	133
Isabelle Whiteley (11)	133
Chantelle Fry (11)	134
Jodie Nicholson (11)	134
Barba Hedley (12)	134
Annabel Kempsey (11)	135
Tabatha Leanne Clark (11)	135
Olivia Towers (11)	135

Phoenix School

Georgina Mannering (12)	136
Yasmin Sangha (12)	136
Hannah Fowles (13)	137
Jack Evans (12)	137
Lauren Cox (12)	138
Stefan Ecclestone (12)	138
Daniel Benting (12)	139
Nathan Musgrave (13)	139
Chris Johnson (12)	140
April Morris (13)	140
Lewis Hocking (11)	141
Shannon Tranter (11)	141
Jessica Hayward (13)	142
Danielle Antonsen (11)	142
Emily Buttery (12)	143
Nathan Wilkinson (11)	143
Ben Folger (12)	144
Stephanie Jean Rippon (11)	144
Natasha Griffin (12)	145
Gemma Machin (11)	145
Laura Oliver-Day (12)	146
Rosie May (13)	146
Kyle Perry (11)	146
Robert Leigh (13)	147
Aimee Glover (13)	147
Samantha Mathars (12)	147
Andrew Thorpe (12)	148

Amy Huntington (13)	149
William Davies (13)	150
Kirsty Edwards (12)	150
Ryan Cooke (11)	151
Luke Antonsen (12)	151
Lewis Hayward (11)	152
Haydn Coates (11)	152
Georgia Gadd (12)	152
Thomas Byrne (11)	153
Rachel Smith (13)	153
Ashley Kitson (12)	153
Laura Greenfield (13)	154
Laura Onions (13)	154
Danielle Horton (11)	155
Sam Holding (11)	155
Alexander Edwards (12)	156
Tom Seymour (13)	156
Alexander Edwards (12)	157
Lyndsey Pitchford	157
Nicole Dickenson (12)	158
Sophie Needle (12)	158
Alex Hallewell (12)	159
Erika Peake (12)	159
Harriet Blower (12)	160
Jodie Hewitt (12)	160
Kristy Williams (13)	161
Rebekah Hughes (12)	161
Jamie Wynn (12)	162
Jessica Jarvis (12)	162
Gavin Brooks (12)	163
Josh Weale (11)	163
Jodie Hayward (12)	164
Natalie James (11)	165
Jodie Thomas (12)	166
Sophie Price (11)	166
Ahmed Hussain (13)	167
Laura Edwards (11)	167
Rachel Maddocks (12)	168
William Bradley (12)	168
Reiss Sudden (12)	169
Christopher Weavill (12)	169
Scott Peters (13)	170

Liam Wilkinson (11)	170
Kieren Griffin (12)	171
Josh Robinson (11)	171
Ryan Trowers (11)	172
Michael McCallin (13)	172
Tom Boneham (13)	173
Lewis Bates (12)	173
Courtney Newdell (12)	174
Leah Perry (11)	175
Alex Tarpey (11)	176
Matthew Russell (11)	177
Emma Childs (13)	178
David Rodrigues (11)	178
Rebecca Mottershaw (12)	179

Sundorne School

Sally Pugh (11)	179
Gareth Price (11)	180
Cerys Pardy (11)	180
Daniel Lloyd (11)	181
Jack Price (11)	181
Kelly Tipton (11)	182
Scott Mammone (11)	182
Bethan Williams (11)	183
Rachel Hanson (11)	183
Andrew Jackson (11)	184
Emma Davis (12)	184
Daniel Francis (11)	185
Timothy Gulliver (11)	185
Amy Good (11)	186
Erin Steen (11)	186
Melissa McIntyre (11)	187
Stephen Lilico (11)	187
Neil Guy (11)	188
Hannah McGonagle (11)	188
Holly Pardoe (11)	189
Katie Griffiths (11)	189
Corinne Jones (12)	190
Steven Lewis (11)	190
Lauren Hosking (12)	191
Daniel Howells (11)	191

Joshua Steer (11)	192
Demi Roberts (11)	192
Abigail Groome	193
Daniel Briscoe (11)	193
Ben Roberts (12)	194
Lisa Gibson (11)	194
Scott Hopkinson (11)	195
Zoe Charles (11)	195
Naomi White (11)	196
Josh Evans (11)	197
Stacey Price (11)	198
Liam Thomas (12)	199
Ryan Davies (11)	200
Robyn Hughes (11)	200
Ryan Owen (11)	201
Samuel Rust (11)	201
Ashley Mitchell (11)	202
Summer Robertson (11)	202
Jamie Roberts (11)	203
Thomas Butler (11)	203
Michael Bufton (12)	204
Abi Kelly (12)	204
Jodie Brown (11)	205
Karl Davies (11)	205
Tara Broadhurst (11)	205
Jade Titley (11)	206

Thomas Telford School

Kate Marshall (12)	206
Daniel Codling (13)	207
Louise Kealy (11)	207
Ashley Wilkes (11)	208
Charley Williams (12)	208
Joseph Cox (11)	209
Amraj Reehal (11)	209
Matthew Poole (12)	210
Lara Vail (11)	210
Rhys Simmonds (11)	211
Tom Yeo (11)	211
Grace Lamsdale (12)	212
Natasha Martin-Shaw (11)	212

Mitchell Norman (12)	213
Rebecca Cooper (12)	213
Jamie Mackenzie (12)	214
Harry Lewis (11)	214
Kirsty Jones (13)	215
Joanna Foster (11)	215
Molly Clarke (12)	216
Aoife Kelly (11)	216
Marie Myler (11)	217
Tom Haynes (11)	217
Emma Sutton (12)	218
Chelsea Norris (12)	219
Matthew Squires (11)	220
Thomas De Vere (12)	220
Cassie Lindley (11)	221
Alexandra Burton (11)	221
Gemma Wells (11)	222
Daniel Goodall (12)	222
Kelsie Fall (12)	223
Grace Atkinson (11)	223
Louisa Piller (12)	224
Bethany Carter (12)	224
Fraser Grieve (11)	225
Laura Bailey (13)	225
Thomas Williams (12)	226
Jordan Griffiths (11)	227
George Jones (12)	228
Jodie Brown (11)	228
Unnas Nadeem (12)	229
Emma Murray (11)	229
Maddison McNally (11)	230
Oliver Woodhouse (11)	230
Mitchell Hill (11)	231
Megan Ward (12)	231
Kinnery Patel (11)	232
Louise Pritchard (12)	232
Carly-Jade Newnes (11)	233
Oliver Strothers (11)	233
Laurence Newman (11)	234
Jane Driscoll (11)	234
Sean Graham (11)	235
Dean Richardson (11)	235

Joshua Whaites (11)	236
Olivia Walsh (11)	236
Steven Copp (11)	237
Nicola Martin (11)	237
Reece Smith (11)	238
Joshua Rogers (11)	238
Mohammed Qureshi (12)	239
Jessica Tonks (11)	239
Emma Irwin (11)	240
David Pickering (11)	240
Rebecca Percox (11)	241
Rachael Holyhead (11)	241
Tajinder Poonian (11)	242
Jessica Haynes (11)	242
Rachael Kenny (11)	243
Daniel Aston (11)	243
Thomas Collier (11)	244
Connor Goldson (11)	244
Dafydd Francis (12)	245
Victoria Green (12)	245
Nicholas Lane (11)	246
Curtis Goodman (11)	246
Lewis Sedgley (12)	247
Chloe Simister (11)	247
Bobby Standley (12)	248
Poppy Bennett (13)	249
Charlotte Housden (12)	250
Jamie Hannah (12)	250
Chloe French (11)	251
Gina Tarantonio (12)	251
Jesica Beaumont (12)	252
Shawnee Blackmore (12)	252
Nicola Kerr (11)	253
Erin Davies (12)	253
Natalie Hope (12)	254
Sukhvinder Gill (11)	254
Lois Perkins (12)	255
Matthew Jones (11)	255
Becki White (12)	256
Kate Breeze (11)	257
James McIntyre (13)	258
Amelia Reynolds (13)	258

Christopher Newbury (11)	259
Lucy Poole (11)	259
Tara Grant (11)	260
Joshua Reynolds (11)	260
Alex Liversage (12)	261
Andrew Stewart (11)	261
Claire Brown (11)	262
Emma Tranter (11)	262
Jack Collier (11)	263
Salli-ann Mathews (11)	263
Charlotte Armstrong (12)	264
Joel Hibbert (11)	264
Jessica Skinner (12)	264
Lucy Coles (11)	265
Keesha Carpenter (11)	265
Robin Allard (11)	265
Kalpna Ahir (12)	266
Matthew Pacey (11)	266
Samuel Deakin (11)	266
Abigail Cooper (12)	267
Kerry Lancaster (12)	267

The Poems

Butterfly, Butterfly!

Butterfly, butterfly flying around
Never, never hitting the ground.

Always fluttering round and about,
Almost certainly never in doubt.

Butterfly, butterfly floating up high
High, high in the sky.

Always bobbing up and down,
Flying, floating round and round.

Butterfly, butterfly landing on a flower
Standing as tall as a tower.

Always standing, flapping wings,
Not knowing what the next day brings.

Danielle Groves (12)
Abraham Darby School

The Night Wolf

My silver eyes shine in the moonlight,
My grey fur glowing while I examine the scenery
My fangs as sharp as a rocky boulder.
My muscles tense as my prey comes near.

The moon at mid sky.
I sleep in the day and prowl at night.
I'm all alone, my friends have gone.
There's no one with me, no one to care.
My mother doesn't care for me.

The sun comes out
And I . . . seek freedom.

Shane Payne (12)
Abraham Darby School

Hail United

Exciting atmosphere
Hail United
Rooney is the *best!*
We're over the moon 'cause,
We got the Roon.

Exciting atmosphere
Hail United
We are the best
Better than the rest.

Exciting atmosphere
Hail United
We are the best
Arsenal goes and hides in their nest.

We have a captain
Who is the best
His game is mean
His name is *Keane.*

Chris Pettitt (12)
Abraham Darby School

New York

People as small as you and me.
Crime is always to be seen
Tall buildings stand proud, taxis racing up and down.
Packed with streets left and right
Up and down.
Outstanding buildings far and wide
Noise we hear night and day.
Full of monuments in every way
This big city has everything you can think of
New York.

Stewart Boffey (12)
Abraham Darby School

Where Am I?

Everywhere is loud
All day long,
Bells are going
All day long,
Gloomy as frost
All day long,
Balls are bouncing
All day long,
Smell of fire
All day long,
Delicious food
All day long,
Pupils chatting
All daylong.
Where am I?

Danielle Spencer (12)
Abraham Darby School

Mothers

She may scream and shout,
But I don't care.
She is loving and caring,
Also she is fair.

Best with my homework,
Gives me money,
Very good at art and also,
Very funny.

She is very very tidy
She never makes a mess.
She looks after the kids,
And thinks I'm the best.

Charlotte Elvin (11)
Abraham Darby School

Who Am I?

Am I a bird
Disappearing behind a cloud
Or am I a dancer
Spinning round and round?

Am I the wind
Passing through trees
Or am I the seasons
For the winter breeze?

Am I a crystal
Glistening like a star
Or am I a plane
Going far?

Am I a light bulb
Lighting up a room
Or am I a mummy
In a dusty tomb?

Am I a baby
Learning to walk
Or am I a duck
That squawks?

Am I a box
Filled with toys
Or am I a guitar
That makes noise?

Am I a scented candle
That smells
Or am I any of these things?
Who can tell?

Sarah Smith (12)
Abraham Darby School

Motherly Love

My mum's name is Veda
She is the leader,
She does my dinner and tea,
She does special things for me.
She cleans and tidies the house,
She scurries around like a mouse.
She's in the bath after me,
In there an hour or three.
Always doing her hair,
And doesn't even care.
Dresses young at heart,
Always looks very smart,
She always makes me laugh,
She's the best mum I could have.
She watches all the soaps on TV,
Sits and watches movies with me,
She stays up till quite late at night,
To make sure everything is alright.
Depending if we have to go far,
She will drive us around in the car.
She spends hours each day washing and drying clothes
Wonders where they all come from, no one knows.
She doesn't take it as a joke,
When she has to fix things that are broke.
If your bedroom is a tip
Don't expect to go on a trip.
If the washing-up has not been done,
Don't expect to have any fun
I love my mum
She is so fun.

Hannah Griffiths (12)
Abraham Darby School

Pop Stars

They dress up like a really posh queen,
In short pink dresses,
And high heel things,
But are always in a limousine.

But then there are the men,
Who look like Barbie's Ken
With leather trousers,
And always have the new trend.

Kiddie pop stars prance around,
With their mansion full of toys,
And their squeaky little voices.

But we all know that pop stars,
Are all the same,
Perfect and pretty,
Making everyone go insane.

Wanting to look like pop stars,
Is just one thing we can't all do,
Cause if you want to be a spoilt brat
Then that is totally up to you.

Natalie Edwards (12)
Abraham Darby School

France A Place Of Magic

France is a place of beauty and peace,
As you walk through the stone-cobbled streets
A strong scent of fresh bread hits you,
The Eiffel Tower soars over all the other houses,
It is almost like the eye of Paris,
As you look over into the countryside
All you see is rows of orchards,
France is home of some of the finest and sweetest wines
                                    around today.

Daniel Onions (12)
Abraham Darby School

The School Is A Prison

The school is a prison
It's where I am trapped,
I used to be sane
But now I have snapped.

This school is a prison
Bars surround it,
Until all the teachers leave
In their big, fancy cars.

This school is a prison
The grounds are a mess
With the help of a cleaner
The rubbish would be less.

The school is a prison
It makes me stressed
The uniform's so yucky
I can hardly get dressed.

This school is a prison
The problems they weave,
But then I remember
Not long till I leave.

Faye Edwards & Jamie Smith (15)
Abraham Darby School

A Poem About Anthony

White skin as cold as ice
Roughly 4 foot 11
Blue eyes as bright as the sky
Brown hair as dark as the night sky
And has feet as big as a mile high in the sky
Wears glasses, the lenses as thin as a sheet of ice.
And as tall as a lamp post with an illuminous light.

Patrick Matthews (12)
Abraham Darby School

Tarantula

The hairy, scary tarantula
Well it's not so scary after all.
It's scared of you and me
Cuz we're the big, ugly monsters
It won't hurt me.
With its 8 legs
It crawls upon your knee
With its little 8 eyes
It can see
Its soft, breakable web
It hangs from the wall
And then you notice
It's above your head
And you flee in fear
The hairy, scary tarantula
It wouldn't hurt me!

Sophie Olver (13)
Abraham Darby School

Foxy

Hairy foxes
Don't stuff them in cardboard boxes,
They sometimes get in a mood
And they hunt their food
Their teeth are sharp
They should try playing a harp
Sometimes they're lazy,
They smell like a daisy.
They sometimes get into a fight,
They like to sleep at night.

Sudeep Singh (12)
Abraham Darby School

Man Utd

Man Utd are the best
They're better than all the rest
Watch them score and score and score
More and more and more.

Lots of boys
With some new toys
Watching lots of matches
And goalies' catches.

Listen to the crowds cheer
Do you know who drank the beer?
Man Utd are the best
They're better than all the rest.

Go Man Utd!

Kerry Clarke (11)
Abraham Darby School

The Moon

The moon could rust
The moon has dust
The moon is cold
The moon is gold
The moon is crazy
The moon is a daisy
The moon is a crater
We collect data
The moon
Is in outer space
We have a database.

Amy Trewartha (12)
Abraham Darby School

My Best Friend

Lauren is my friend,
And has long hair,
Natural highlights,
But she doesn't care.

She has big teeth,
But a lovely smile,
We broke up once,
But only for a while.

She's a real sporty girl,
With a trumpet in her hand,
Her greatest aim,
Is to be part of a band.

We met in the nursery,
And have since been friends,
Hopefully our friendship will be going,
Until my life ends.

Rebecca Powell (12)
Abraham Darby School

David Beckham

When he scored for Man United
The crowd and the players were delighted,
Now he plays for Real Madrid,
He doesn't score and plays like a kid.

He has got two kids and a wife,
Who used to be called Posh Spice,
One of his kids is named after a place,
The other is named after a Shakespeare ace.

When he is injured on the floor,
He gets back up and goes for more,
When he scores he scores in style,
But he hasn't scored in a while.

Shaun Coldicutt (11)
Abraham Darby School

The Shivers

If you want me to haunt your house
And loudly scream your name
If you want me to shake your bed
And fill your head with shame.

If you want me to drive you insane
And call you nasty names
If you want me to rattle your brain
And cause you lots of pain.

If you want me to go through walls
And rock your house at night
If you want me to smash your plates
And give you a big fright.

If you want me to float around
And haunt your mum and dad
If you want me to rattle my chains
And make your life so sad.

If you want me to do these things
Then whisper three times at night
'The phantom
The phantom
The phantom.'

James Pilling (11)
Abraham Darby School

The Sun

Sun, sun so high in the sky
Shining so brightly
Above the stars
Sun at night is very sparkly
The sun is one of the stars
Sun, it's bedtime now
Your friend, Moon is here.

Zahid Reza (12)
Abraham Darby School

A Person I Know

The person I know is,
My cousin Jonathan,
He likes playing football,
And when I go round we have a ball.

He lives in Stirchley,
And has a dog called Bounty,
He has two sisters,
And goes to Ab Dab, the best school in the county.

He plays on his Xbox,
And is twelve years old,
He also likes cars,
And his house isn't very cold.

He supports Man United
When he watches them he gets excited,
He has all the shirts,
And when they win he is delighted.

Thomas Managh (11)
Abraham Darby School

Wayne Rooney

I like Wayne Rooney he is the best
He is better than all the rest
I think he is great
I don't care what everybody says,
When he scores the crowd goes wild
I watch all his games and they don't let him down
That's why I like him,
This year he is not going down
He is going to make everybody wear a crown
And he will be sitting on the throne
And will be king of the year.

Nathan Moore (11)
Abraham Darby School

Spooky Stories

If you want me to shake your bed
And float around your room
If you want me to blow a breeze
And bring your house to doom.

Then whisper for me with all your might
And whisper this three times at night,
'The phantom
The phantom
The phantom.'

If you want me to kill your dad
And murder your mummy
If you want me to haunt your bro
And rumble your tummy.

Then wish for me with all your might
And whisper this three times at night,
'The phantom
The phantom
The phantom.'

If you want me to haunt your house
And give you such a fright
If you want me to shake your curtains
And give you a bad bite.

Then wish for me with all your might
And whisper this three times at night,
'The phantom
The phantom
The phantom.'

Lauren Price (11)
Abraham Darby School

My Big Brother

When my brother is at home,
He hides behind the wall,
And waits for me to walk past,
And then he throws his ball.

It hits me on the head
And then he shouts, *'Score!'*
He starts to laugh,
As if he likes it more.

I run down to Mum,
He climbs in his fancy car,
I shout to him
But he's gone too far.

When it's dark,
And everyone has gone to bed,
He sits in his room,
Bouncing a ball on his head.

Candice Smith (11)
Abraham Darby School

My Best Friend Emma Tucker

My best friend is Emma Tucker
Not just because she is a real good looker.

I think that she will really go far
Because she is my wonder star.

I hope and pray everyday she will be there
For me all the way.

I will be her friend right until the very end
She might be annoying but aren't all friends like that
She has a real big heart and that is that.

Parês Thomas (11)
Abraham Darby School

The Phantom!

If you want me to drag my chains
And touch you with cold hands.

If you want me to slam your door
And smash your pots and pans.

Then wish for me with all your might and
Whisper this three times at night,
>'The Phantom!
>The Phantom!
>The Phantom!'

If you want me to walk through walls and give your dad a fright.

Then wish for me with all your might
And whisper this three times at night,
>'The Phantom!
>>The Phantom!
>>>The Phantom!'

Robert Wenlock (11)
Abraham Darby School

Lunch

As silent as a mouse,
As sneaky as a thief,
The snake slithered towards its prey,
It came up on the mouse as it trembled in fear,
The snake struck at it but missed,
Then glared at the mouse with an evil sign of enjoyment,
Slithering off looking for its prey the snake finally found its victim,
And suddenly that sinister look reappeared on its face,
And with all its might it struck at its prey,
And with that blow it brought its lunch to the ground,
Constricting his meal into a mass of crushed bones,
At last the snake was triumphant!

Matthew Burrows (12)
Abraham Darby School

Angel

Up above the fluffy white clouds,
In a quiet delicate land,
Of angels and imps
All the words you hear
Throughout the day
Are the tunes of the gentle band
The twinkling of the stars
Are their halos glowing?
The horrible miserable rain
Is their tears because someone
Has upset them
By taking their beauty for granted.
Between their silky wings
Is a pot of silver snow
Ready to sprinkle on a beautiful young person
And that person
. . . is you, dear friend.

Chelsea Lowe (11)
Abraham Darby School

My Best Friend

Thoughtful and loyal,
She makes me laugh as much as anyone would,
Great personality,
Helps me with homework more than anyone else could.

You can tell her a secret and she won't tell,
If I need her to, she will stick by me all the way,
If I fall over she'll help,
If you don't have money she will pay.

Tammy Muddell (12)
Abraham Darby School

Rose

Way upon a tree so high lies a rose
Dancing in the sky.

Red, red silk,
And petals of steel,
Has the best silky feel.

Valentine and heartbreak
Lightly floating on a lake holds problems for all
Some big and some small.

Colour to kiss
And colour to cuddle
Usually find me in a huddle.
Loving red
And
Warmly said,
'I love you'.

Siân Smith (12)
Abraham Darby School

Snake

The smooth skin of something in a ring hissing at me,
All I could see was a bright red tongue waiting to get me,
It moved fast
It was the size of a skipping rope,
I could feel it looking me in the eyes,
It slithered towards me,
I could feel its cold and dry skin coming up my legs
Then my whole life came to an end.

Carla Rann (12)
Abraham Darby School

The Whale Song

Thick black clouds of oil flood the silent seas,
Mournful cries echo around me,
I look above and see the dark shadow of a killer boat.
A long sharp glinting object pierces the heart of the whale
                                                                         closest to me
He takes his final breath and slowly drifts to the bottom of the ocean.
I shout to the whales, there's no reply
I glance down to the dead whale and hope I'm not next
The ocean is silent
The ocean is dead.

Kirsty Colclough (11)
Abraham Darby School

Ivy

Ivy is her name
She smells like a rose
She's as soft as a panda
But when I look up she's all I can see
I love you Ivy
Like you love me.

Scott Brough (14)
Abraham Darby School

Rabbit!

He's small and fluffy and very cute,
He has big feet and loves to eat,
He has lots of fur and a very pink nose,
He has long floppy ears he doesn't have fears,
He loves being free because he is just like me!
Mopsy!

Katie O'Hanlon (12)
Abraham Darby School

Sly Snakes

Curled up in a ball there it will stay
Till danger passes then he will be on his way
Curled up like a stone silent and still
Waiting yes waiting for his kill.
His beady little eyes hissing goodnight
He will be hanging there all throughout the night!
His skin twinkles in the light
I feel sorry for the little mouse running past that night!

Tara Atterbury (12)
Abraham Darby School

The Owl

The owl was flying through the night
Spotting mice with pinpoint sight
Silent gliding in gusty trees
Its wings held upon the midnight breeze
It spies its prey way down below
Feathers white in moonlight glow
Steel claws grab a tiny mouse
Taking it back to the old barn house.

Daniel Heaword (12)
Abraham Darby School

Foxes

Foxes, foxes, great big foxes
Lying around in great big boxes
With heads poking out from every direction,
Waiting and waiting for their prey to come out,
Suddenly a pounce of a twelve-ounce fox
Tearing and wearing out their prey.

Hayley Watton (12)
Abraham Darby School

I'm Not Going To School Today . . .

'I'm not going to school today,'
Said defiant little Danny
'It's supposed to be a lot of fun,
But I'm not having any!'

The teacher keeps on asking questions,
And it's clear for all to see,
She doesn't know the answers
Cus she keeps on asking me!

After sitting deep in thought
Danny jumped up with glee,
'I think I'll go after all,
Cus teacher might need me!'

Danny Perkins (12)
Abraham Darby School

My Brothers

My brothers are funny
And are good to talk to
They can solve problems
And they like me too.

My brothers can tell jokes
Like no one knows
One can cook really well
As I well know.

My brothers are good they are so great
They can help me in tough spots
And hate the things that I hate
And they're my brothers; they're there to stay
So other people keep away.

Christopher Baxter (12)
Abraham Darby School

New York

New York is a city that never sleeps,
It is on the edge of the country,
There are one million people in the city,
It is a dot on the map.

New York is a city infested by crime,
But in the city there are some cops,
Law is a fading light in the darkness,
But it is still going strong.

The sky is so clear it is like fresh water,
The skyscrapers poke right into the sky,
The Statue of Liberty is a well-known symbol,
But the city can be noisy.

Luke Underwood (13)
Abraham Darby School

Life

Life is like a jigsaw puzzle,
That is so big,
If you stood in the middle,
You would never see the corners.

Life is like a jigsaw puzzle,
That is so hard
If you tried to work it out,
The pieces would never fit together.

Life is like a puzzle,
That refuses to fit together.

Life is like a puzzle
That can't be worked out.

This is life.

Oliver Yardley (12)
Abraham Darby School

My Dog Meg

My dog Meg has a black and white coat
She has big, floppy ears and a small tail,
Which she wags about like mad.
Around her neck she wears a thick blue collar
With a golden tag saying *Meg*.
She walks around like she owns the place
She is bred to hunt rabbits, pheasants and pigeons.
She is the greatest dog anyone could have.

Alex Bridgwater (12)
Abraham Darby School

About My Mum

My mum has big blue eyes which,
Sparkle in the night,
But she has really good eyesight
She has one golden tooth,
She doesn't like us on the roof
She always has a smile on her face
But the problem is she's always on our case
But she calls me her little star.

Natalie Resoun (13)
Abraham Darby School

Foxes

A fox is soft and furry
They make you feel warm
They have a bushy tail
They also have red hair
They have two pointy ears
They have a big long nose.

James Powis (12)
Abraham Darby School

My Brother Graham

He is as tall as a giant,
He is taller than you or me.

His eyes glisten through the seas,
Better than yours or mine do.

When we have fun,
That's when his hair shines like the sun.

His freckles are like diamonds,
They sparkle through the islands.

Jayne Collis (12)
Abraham Darby School

My Grandad

My grandad is very small like me,
He used to be a hippy,
The glasses he wears are small like his eyes,
Yet his ears are like pudding pies,
His head is almost going bald,
His reason is he's kind of old.
Wherever he is he's looking smart,
His job is teaching people how to drive a van,
The only problem is he's married to my nan.

Katherine Evans (12)
Abraham Darby School

Night Stars

S tar light, star bright
T ip of the moon behind the cloud
A hhh watching the fireworks
R ockets flying high in the sky
S tar light, star bright.

Charlotte Wade (12)
Abraham Darby School

Untitled

London is a great big attraction
Labour Party is always in action,
The London Eye is a great place to visit,
Biggest Ferris wheel in Europe isn't it
It's always the host of lots of premiers
And sometimes the place is full of scares,
This place in our country is very popular
All people in the world can come by car,
This is London, it's very funny
And is a perfect place to spend your money.

Damien Griffiths (12)
Abraham Darby School

WWE

Atmosphere feeling ten times
Bigger than any world cup
Fireworks brighter than daylight.
These fireworks could drown out a festival
Chanting and banging as loud
As one hundred school bands
Arena that seems the same size as a country.

Oliver Rimmer (12)
Abraham Darby School

Wembley

The stands of the Wembley stadium are red and white,
    as bright as fire
The turf is soft and green like a sponge,
The jackets of the police illuminate the stadium
And the two white towers are as white as the clouds,
You can hear the hooligans roar as loud as thunder
And the echoes of the English fans shake the ground of Wembley!
The fans suddenly go quiet as the national anthem is sung.

Jonathan Webster (12)
Abraham Darby School

My Scaredy Friend

He has a sister called Abi and a brother called Mark.
He doesn't mind light, but he's scared in the dark!
We were watching TV; he slept at my house,
But then he got scared when he saw a mouse!
We went outside and he saw the rake,
But jumped out of his skin, he thought it was a snake!
Then he went to my pond; he liked it there,
There were no snakes, or mice, or bears,
The peace only lasted for a while,
He thought he saw a crocodile!
He was so scared, we had to call his dad,
He was the scarediest friend I ever had.

Alexander Durnall (11)
Abraham Darby School

My Cousin Tom

My cousin Tom acts real cool
But I just think he acts a fool
With his gold chains and his Rockport shoes
His expensive rings and his bottles of booze.

With his stylish hair and his piles of cash
His smart clothes and his miniature tash
He thinks he's big and he thinks he's ace
But when he reads this, you wanna see his face.

Liam Baldi (13)
Abraham Darby School

The Alien Man

The ginormous nose, wet as a frog
Manky toenails,
Annoying as a fly,
His chubby butt in the sky
The alien man knows why.

Chris Trafford (12)
Abraham Darby School

My Best Friend Laura

Laura is my friend
With welcoming brown eyes,
A great sense of humour,
And she hardly ever sighs.

My friend Laura
Is a year younger than me,
She is a great drawer
And gives me company.

We mainly meet at dance school,
Which we attend most days a week,
Our mums are best friends too,
And our sisters hide-and-seek.

We fall out occasionally,
But it's only very brief,
After a day or two,
We turn a new leaf.

We both have little sisters,
Who are also best friends,
They have many arguments,
With many twists and bends.

We met when we were one,
And have been friends since then.
Played in our gardens,
And made a big den.

Eleanor Ballinger (11)
Abraham Darby School

The Woods By My House

The woods by my house are beautiful
In the spring as the blossom blooms with all its glory.
The woods by my house looks scary and sinister in the autumn
As the leaves fall and the wind blows
As if it were a chilling whisper in the evening breeze

The woods by my house look comforting and peaceful in the summer
As the birds fly and the butterflies flutter
From the roses near the old oak tree.

The woods by my house look like a white blanket
Covering the leafless branches of the trees,
And the frost that makes the grass go crispy, yet soft with snow.

Alex Fallon (13)
Abraham Darby School

Parents

Thou tries so hard to cheer me when I'm sad,
Helped me through those times when I was alone,
And thou art kind when I have been so bad,
When I have looked at thee as cold as stone.

Thou dost work to get our family money,
Thou put together my broken bunk bed
When we cry thou laughs and is so funny,
Then saws together pine wood in the shed.

Thou washes all my clothes to make them clean,
Nails shelves to my wall so I say thank you,
Sewing up our ripped clothes with the machine,
And explain the things that we look blank to.

This letter is merely a thank you note,
For the very best parents I do vote.

Bethany Gentempo (12)
Meole Brace School

The Oak Tree

The grey squirrel scurried off,
Clutching the acorn.
Stopped,
Buried it.

The squirrel never returned
Silent and still
The seeds lay there
Until one day,
A weak green shoot poked out
A sign of life.

The tree grew
Until it was a healthy sapling.
Spreading its thin toes
Down into the rich earth,
Absorbing moisture like a thirsty buffalo.

Soon the oak towered
Over all the flowers
Woodpeckers foraged for food
Children played
All night and day.

Many years later
The tree died
It left behind an acorn;
Ready to take its place.

Joseph Ruxton (13)
Meole Brace School

Undercover

There once was a man called Clive,
He worked for MI5,
He took a shot in the head,
But he wasn't dead,
And was back out the very next day, alive.

Neil Love (13)
Meole Brace School

Dancer

Each day every day
I wake up in the morning
Go to school come home.

I'm misunderstood
My life is a routine
Without any music.

There's just one small thing,
A tiny glimmer of light
That I hold on to

I dance

I dance in my dreams
And I dance under the lights
My sanctuary.

Each step carries me
Further from the miseries
Of reality.

I'm lost in my world
All by myself
Where my wishes come true and I set the rules.

I live for this time when nothing else matters
My freedom
The time when I'm alive.

Dancing is my life
This is my one true passion
My retreat

It is my small thing
That tiny glimmer of light
Which I hold on to,

Where do I live?
Here . . .
I dance.

Lucia James (13)
Meole Brace School

The Game

He sits on the window ledge,
His ears pricked up,
His eyes open wide.

His body as still as frozen ice,
When *whoosh whoosh*
His tail flicks from side to side.

His eyes still fixed on something in the grass,
He crouches down,
And waits.

He waits
He waits
Until the grass rustles and he's off.

He plummets through the air,
His eyes still fixed on the grass,
He lands softly and waits.

He starts rushing through the grass,
Twisting and turning,
He stops.

His head turns this way and that,
His paws go up and down,
He's got his prey.

To him nothing in this world matters right now,
Except for the challenge,
Of his game.

Jenny Collins (13)
Meole Brace School

Burning Blossoms

Burning blossoms hang,
Trembling in the slight, warm breeze;
Forever to fall.

Liam Shaw (13)
Meole Brace School

Feta Cheese

Oh, feta cheese, thy creamy soft flavour
Eternally do I crave thy taste.
For thou I risk dangerous labour
And hurry to shops in mesmerised haste.

Turning salads, bland into masterpieces
Lightly coated in they refreshing salt brine,
I covet thine perfectly formed creases
And wish to make thee eternally mine.

From the lands of Greece, thou hast come for me
And bestowed thy virtues upon my bread
As I woke this morning, my mind still dreaming
Of thoughts for feta inside my head.

Oh, feta cheese, thou hast enriched my life
And if a woman, thou wouldst be my wife.

Sam Kenney (12)
Meole Brace School

To Cream

Oh for thy smooth and foaming texture
Cream poured upon one's tasteless cake,
Hath made it rich and divinest mixture,
No longer now's unpalatable bake.

Oh for thine thickest batch of Heaven
My taste buds fight with starving hunger,
Earth's finest thing hath been brought by Devon,
Yes clotted cream's what's made me stronger.

But let's not forget thine's whipped sensation
With scones or jam on one's cherry bun,
I've craved thy taste with expectation
For it lengthens all days 'til eating I've done.

For me, for cream I toast to Elmlea,
Sit back in my chair and feast with glee.

Quentin Otto (13)
Meole Brace School

Searching

It was like when you have been searching all night,
I am shattered every day,
I have been searching all night,
In the very black of night.

I am nearly there, like a fox chasing rabbits,
I am so close,
I want to see you, like watching you on stage,
I am almost there,
I can feel you breathe.

I have found you!
I have found you!
I will never leave you,
Like vines up a wall,
We are twisted together.

Megan Williams (12)
Meole Brace School

The Shadow

My face half cast in the shadow
As I stand and weep
I'm left in the shadow
So my tears can't be seen spilt afresh on the concrete
And I can see the light
But still I'm stranded by the dark
And that light seems so close
But yet so far.
So many walk by,
Without even a glance
Oh, they notice the shadow,
But not me and my weeping stance
So lord, please come down and end this eternal night
Ease my pain
And let me bathe in that heavenly light.

Danny Williams (15)
Meole Brace School

Confusion Day

Confusion day is the strangest day,
Where everything seems to be wrong.
You never know where or what you are,
And nothing is where it belongs.

Some people think they are warthogs,
While others prefer to be cows,
But the strangest of people just sit on church steeples,
Singing, 'Gup-gup gazookle, guttzow!'

On confusion day, all the grass turns pink,
And the sky turns green instead of blue.
The pigs grow wings and the ducks say, 'Ping,'
And the sheep instead of baa say, 'Moo.'

Confusion day will be your strangest day,
When it comes, everything will be wrong.
You won't know where, who or what you are,
And you won't know where you belong.

Tim Farrow (11)
Meole Brace School

The Train

As the train drives in all the figures start moving,
But me? I just stand still, staying low,
Exchanging places from platform to train,
But me? I just stand still, staying low,
Someone nearly knocks me, as they rush on to the train.
But me? I just stand still, staying low,
The whistle goes, and the train departs
But me? I just stand still, staying low,
In comes number 13 and stops at my platform
But me? I just stand still, staying low,
Remembering that train, from all those years ago,
When it didn't stop at all.
Knocking me down with a blow.

Shannon Mosley (13)
Meole Brace School

Mum's Sonnet

You have always been there and kind to me,
When ill, you care, make me better again.
One day I hope to repay you, you see.
I'll say again, never have thou felt pain.

Friends are close but you are closer, always.
Thou shall ne'er leave thee for eternity
When you're gone I miss thee, counting the days.
Until you have returned, wilful and free.

In this modern world we argue sometimes
We squabble over things, silly, unwise,
I feel you hate me so, beneath the lies.
I sit in my room unhappy, thou cries.

Can you please forgive me, always be friends
I'll stick by your side together 'til end.

Jade Colley (12)
Meole Brace School

The Moon
(A sonnet)

Thou place that no man can go to alone
Up there so far away in endless space
Thy hard and strong as if made by grey stone
Thou craters look as if they are a face
Few people know how it feels to be there
So few people know if the myths are true
I look up at the pretty moon and stare
Wondering if it is just cream or blue
I dream of being a great astronaut
To be able to float around so free
Oh why is it so far away? I thought.
To be there, oh amazing it would be
It looks too big to be able to float
How cold is thy? Would I need my big coat?

Rebecca Lawn (13)
Meole Brace School

Nature Rhythm
(A sonnet)

The beautiful swaying leaves on thy trees,
Blossoming bluebells tall under thou sun,
As graceful is the motion of the three,
Birds overhead, frolicking, having fun.

As the day closes, thy night upon us,
Everything is sheltered under thy shade,
All the plants grow tall with minimum fuss
Their shimmering shadows begin to fade.

Morning dew upon the vast fields glisten,
As one gazes up at the clear blue sky,
Hearing the buzzing bees when you listen,
You see butterflies flutter gently by.

The sun smiling down on the spinning Earth,
The yellow daffodils showing their worth.

Bryony Smith (12)
Meole Brace School

Do Great Minds Think Alike?

It was like when you have been searching all night,
When the answer came to your head:
Do great minds think alike?

If you need a colour to inspire you like
Red, blue or green, look around.

I need you to think awhile, to write a play, a thriller,
                              even if it is very twisted.
Sleep, dream, and let subconscious minds take over
Do great minds think alike?

Paddy Anderson Loake (11)
Meole Brace School

Endless Lake

Drowning in darkness,
Smothered in fear
You cannot see,
And you cannot hear.

The creeping fog,
The crawling clouds
Rolling in,
From all around.

Deafened by thunder
Suffocated alone
As you say,
'It's just the same old drone.'

Paying no attention
And using your hand
I just wanted to talk,
You didn't understand.

The ice is so thick
Too thick to break,
High above me,
In this endless lake.

Fighting for air,
Pulled down too deep,
Memories that I,
Do not want to keep.

Emily Marston (13)
Meole Brace School

The Three Billy Goats Gruff Ballad

The three billy goats gruff,
Lay quietly on the green grass,
Covered in chunks of grey fluff
One was a great ogre of a mass.

The three billy goats gruff wanted to play,
One ran across the bridge it was very big,
Baby ran quickly across, bleating
After he ran he wanted to dig.

The second billy goat gruff
Ran fast and suddenly
Out came big, fat, podgy, ugly, silly troll,
The goats looked up muddled
That troll is really cruel.

The third billy goat gruff
Said, 'Is this your bridge?'
The troll answered, 'It is indeed,'
'But this bridge belongs to a boy called Midge.'
'But this bridge is special, it is where I feed.'

He couldn't believe what he heard,
So he gave him a walloping big kick,
So the goat went back to his herd,
They were upset and he showed them a trick.

Laura Causey (12)
Meole Brace School

Three Little Pigs Ballad

Chorus
The little pigs go through the forest
The wolf starts to watch every move
The pigs have finished and have their rest
And the wolf is feeling very smooth.

'Right pig it is time to go,' said Mother
To the forest they set off,
'I can smell a wolf,' said a brother
Then he found he had a great cough.

Chorus

Then one went up to a nearby farm
Then he used the animals' straw
It took him ages but he stayed calm
The wolf skirted to pounce on the door.

Chorus

The others went with a great saw
So then he cut a huge barn door
Then he started to build his house with straw
But it's no good, it looks such a mess.

Chorus

The third is made out of bricks
Better then his brother's no doubt
Because his is made out of sticks
The wolf awaits to give them a clout.

Chorus

Then the wolf creeps down the chimney
Then the pigs lit the fire
So then the wolf died so grimly
Then it's the end of the little pigs.

Dom Sadd (12)
Meole Brace School

Fairy Tale Ballad

Chorus
Three little pigs so pink and round
They all built different huts with pride
The big bad wolf creeps with no sound
If they went out it would be suicide.

Verse 1
They left to make a living
One built his house out of straw
One built out of sticks for him to live in
The last one built it out of bricks, need I say more.

Chorus

Verse 2
The big bad wolf skulks around in the wood
The big bad wolf saw the hut in which he spied
A pig, which as a lovely feast looks good
He blew the house down to get the pig outside.

Chorus

Verse 3
The pig ran to his brother's hut
The wolf chased fast and saw two pigs
These small brown sticks I will cut
Down came the house so he did lots of gigs.

Chorus

Verse 4
The fleeing pigs get to the hut of bricks
The wolf speeds along to catch his lunch
With his long tongue his lips he licks
One kick, the hut comes down with a crunch.

Chorus

Verse 5
As the hungry wolf went for the kill
As bits of debris fly by
The wolf is certain he will get a fill
The poor little pink pigs must die.

Will Heath (12)
Meole Brace School

Revenge Potion

Skunk's tail: chuck it in first
Nose hairs to make the broth worse
Earwax, toe of a lizard
Stir it up, evil wizard.

Chorus
Simmer, chop, boil and blend
A hand for revenge this potion lends.

Next it's the toenail clippings
Along with a bull's nose ring
Spider's web, saliva of goat
Mix it up, don't let it float.

Chorus

Dead eyeball, through it a pin
Tongue of a fish, bake it in
Hair of those you seek revenge on
Now the charm is good and done.

Chorus

Take a sip of this fatal wine,
For mean revenge it is now time.

Kelli Swancott (13)
Meole Brace School

Football
(A cinquain)

Football
Football crazy
Kick a ball like Beckham
Saha is the team I play for
Kick it!

Nick Jones (11)
Meole Brace School

Love Potion

In the light of red candles
Boil perfume, three samples
Seven drops of deep red wine
I am going to make you mine.

Chorus
In the glass add some soil,
Love and lust quick let's boil.

The feathers of a graceful dove
I make this to feel loved
Stir in oysters and their shells
Soon you'll hear the sound of bells.

Chorus

Round and round the champagne glass
Mix in lips, to make this class.
To make this man love you too,
Add some diamonds just a few.

Chorus

A petal off a red rose
Slivers of his belov'd clothes
A choc'late heart he has bit
Cupid's arrow, now that's it.

Sammy Morris (14)
Meole Brace School

Fishing
(A cinquain)

Fishing
The thrill, fishing
You feel the bite, fishing
You strike the rod and catch a fish,
Fishing.

Jonathan Bunce (12)
Meole Brace School

Why?
(A Sonnet)

Her long dark hair swept across her bowed head,
Moist eyes fixed on the floor, scared to look round,
She wished she could blank out the words they said,
She stood there and to herself she frowned.

She could hear high-pitched giggles looming near,
The moment she dreaded had to arrive,
Her palms were so hot and sticky with fear.
Often she wished that she wasn't alive.

They pulled her hair hard, they stamped on her books,
They showed her no mercy, they didn't care,
From round the hall she spied pitiful looks,
Every day it became harder to bear.

How I wish that life could always be fair,
They had no reason to do this to her.

Sarah Chambers (13)
Meole Brace School

Alone

It was like you had been searching all night!
Stuck in some tunnel of doom
I don't know what on earth I am to do!

I am stuck, I am stuck!
I can't see anything
Not in this horrid black gloominess
Where am I? What am I doing here?
Please get me out! I am suffering . . .

I can't find my way back I am stuck
A tear falling, a twitch calling me
I am stuck, really stuck, forever alone
I whisper quietly a couple of times, 'Twisted! *Twisted!*'

Jazmin Highfield (11)
Meole Brace School

Death Potion Of Evil

Chuck in a bowl of heron wings,
Add the brain of a bird that sings
Mix in a flake of human skin
Let him die from the prick of a pin.

Bubble, bubble, stir this rubble,
Mix the potion or there'll be trouble.

Little toe of a drowned babe goat
Full up lungs of a mad man's throat,
Add some darkness to make this black,
Jet-black tail of a witch's cat.

Bubble, bubble, stir this rubble,
Mix the potion or there'll be trouble.

Mix the mixture till it's all brown,
Add the rim of a dead king's crown
Scale of dragon, claw of a wolf,
Eye of dog ripped by human tool.

Bubble, bubble, stir this rubble,
Mix the potion or there'll be trouble.

Nick Stephens (13)
Meole Brace School

Dads Are Different

Dads are sweet, kind and gentle,
All but mine; he is mental.
Some dads hop, jump and leap,
All mine does is seem to sleep.
Most dads sit, listen and hear,
Mine drinks lots and lots of beer.
All I've said is quite true
But remember Dad I still love you.

Amy Price (13)
Meole Brace School

Death Potion

Throw in a ball of rabbit guts,
In goes a knife that men have cut,
Pour in a bowl of human blood,
Woman's body died in a flood.

Bubble, bubble, that cauldron boil,
Making sure that it does not spoil.

Now the cauldron is turning brown,
We shall make sure that they all drown,
In goes a sword full of men's death,
Next to go is a dead man's breath,
Dropping in is an eagle's wing,
Darkness and death this cauldron brings.

Bubble, bubble, that cauldron boil,
Making sure that it does not spoil.

The deadly poison from a snake,
A deathly pie we shall bake
A black stallion's clean new shoe,
This cauldron shouts, 'Boo, boo, boo,'
In goes a torn and bloody rag,
We are three witches that don't nag.

Bubble, bubble, that cauldron boil,
Making sure that it does not spoil.

Now let's drop in a young deer's horn
Now the small white clothes from a newborn,
Throw in the head of a dead bat,
Now where is that tail off that rat?
This is the end of our small chant,
'Do not tell people.' - 'No we shan't.'

Will Jones (13)
Meole Brace School

Flying Potion

For this potion, first apply
Ingredients to let me fly,
Wing of owl and gosling down
Soft wing beats without a sound.

Simmer carefully, night and day
Then like a bird, fly away.

Honeybees, 300 of
600 wings from up above,
Birch twigs from an old broomstick,
Stir in feathers, mix it quick.

Chorus

Of an eagle, pluck warm heart,
Sparrow's beak killed with a dart,
Add some cloud, and boil it well,
30 eggs from their nest fell.

Chorus

Dissolve in next, rainbow's end,
Butterfly scales to make it blend.
Sing aloud, nightingale song,
Chirp of blackbird, loud and long.

Chorus

Blend in tail of a kite
Then drink this potion, aiding flight.

Chorus

Hannah Morgan (13)
Meole Brace School

A Spell Of Eternal Beauty

A spell for an eternal beauty
To succeed is my duty.

To start two butterfly wings
One of many lovely things.

Chorus
Round about the cauldron go
Singing and dancing as you go.

A cup of morning dew
To make your beauty true.

A scale of an angelfish
Remember your beauty wish.

Chorus

3 grains of silver sand
Wave of a wand in a magic hand.

Add a nightingale's egg
While balancing on one leg.

Chorus

A feather from a white dove
From the Heavens above.

A spoonful of honey
To make it nice and runny.

Chorus

A whisker of a kitten
On which your beauty is written.

The first summer rose
Spread the beauty to your toes.

Chorus

A bunch of cobweb cotton
For all bad looks to be forgotten.

Lily flower, pollen from
Eternal beauty soon will come.

Chorus

A wild strawberry take some juice
That will let the beauty loose.

Add a sprinkle of snowflakes
And that is all the potion takes.

Hannah Swallow (13)
Meole Brace School

Romance's Revenge Potion

Onto the cloth,
Threw legs of moth,
Razor blades,
And from the shade
Steal rott'd newts eyes,
Lover's goodbyes
Then 3 black candles
Light, tonight!

Add a rag doll,
Sound of death toll,
Potted snakes' gizzards
And tooth of blue lizard.
Wood flavoured incense
To make their nerves tense.
Sprinkle elm powder,
Shout to Hecate call her louder!

Boil to broth, and then add your cloth.
Simmer till brown
Add mashed sharks' crown
When potion doth smell
All's good 'n' well
Your revenge is then done
When the clock strikes 10 to 1!

Rebecca Wallen (13)
Meole Brace School

The Hovis Potion

Stir the flour, melt the marge,
Around the bowl to get starch,
Then turn the clock and throw in,
For the potion to really win.
Hair from cook, not two but three,
A Sainsbury's bag to package thee.
A ladle handle to add kick
Half a black spice from old Mick,
Then whisk well with sweat and blood,
Blend it cold with hard baked mud,
Make it clever with witch's hat
Then mash round a mangy old cat.
To finish off with some style,
Add half a nail from brother Kyle,
Now the potion's done and good,
Place it in a house of wood.
Then tap it thrice with your hand
And a loaf of bread will stand!

Matthew Jones (13)
Meole Brace School

The Beatles

I love the Beatles,
Their music blows my mind . . .
And when the floor needs sweeping,
You know that I feel fine.

And when I'm feeling sleepy,
Don't bother me at all . . .
My bass is gently weeping,
I try and play with Paul

So let me introduce to you,
A band I've known for many years . . .
And even in the end,
I'll need you like a friend.

Andy Bullough (13)
Meole Brace School

Pinocchio

Chorus
Pinocchio, he is a wooden boy,
Pinocchio, he is more than a wooden toy.
Gepetto wanted him to be alive,
But wasn't sure if he would survive.

Gepetto made a wooden puppet
With paint and varnish all over,
While the paint and varnish was still wet
With Gepetto's love he was smothered.

Chorus

Gepetto treated him like a real boy
Although he was a wooden toy
Gepetto did all that he could,
Although Pinocchio was made of wood.

Chorus

Pinocchio ends up going to school,
All the teachers made him look like a fool,
He was never any good,
So they chopped him up for firewood.

Robert Cannell (12)
Meole Brace School

The Stars You Never Notice

It was like when you have been searching all night for the stars,
                              but you can never find them.
They are always above you, but only sometimes you notice it.

I am stuck! I am stuck!
The colour of your curtains is bright yellow just like the stars.

They twisted and turned when you tried to pull them across
They never go straight across easily.
Then, you take a glance at the sky and you find the stars!

Emily Robinson (11)
Meole Brace School

Cinderella

Cinderella and her dad lived alone
For years and years they didn't moan
Her lovely dad got married again
Cinderella got left in the rain.

Cinderella washes all day
Her life is turning cloudy grey
Thanks to her two ugly sisters
Her hands are getting covered in blisters.

Cinderella has two ugly sisters
They boss her until she has got blisters
Then an invitation comes through the door
This invitation will be adored.

Cinderella washes all day
Her life is turning cloudy grey
Thanks to her two ugly sisters
Her hands are getting covered in blisters.

Cinderella goes to the ball
Prince's eyes are bigger than a hall
Then suddenly the clock struck 12
Poor old Cinderella has no luck.

Cinderella washes all day
Her life is turning cloudy grey
Thanks to her two ugly sisters
Her hands are getting covered in blisters.

Cinderella got pushed into the door
Cinders is not living anymore
The ugly sister gets a honeymoon
Cinders is going to Heaven soon.

Ashley Titley (12)
Meole Brace School

Cinderella

Cinderella is locked in the house
With only a broom and a pan
Trying to kill a wild mouse
I bet she wished she had a man.

There was a girl called Cinderella
And her mother died painfully
She went to the funeral with an umbrella
She had to wear her normal clothes shamefully.

Her father got remarried
To an evil woman with two ugly daughters
Her clothes is what he had to carry
Then once she fell from a window but he caught her.

Her father was getting beaten up by his wife
They made Cinderella clean up
She tried to kill him with a knife
They even smashed her favourite cup.

Then one day a letter came in the post
Cinderella picked it up
But they wanted it the most
She didn't give it to them so they bashed her up.

The ugly sisters went to the ball
And left Cinderella in the house
Then her fairy godmother arrived in the hall
And made Cinderella go to the ball with a mouse.

When she got there she started dancing with the prince
Whilst the ugly sisters looked in despair
And her father went to eat some mince
A chandelier fell down on the pair.

The chandelier squashed them both
It looked a painful death.

Chris Evans (12)
Meole Brace School

Potion For Complete Mind Control!

Add 3 tears of a crocodile in a blue lagoon.
Blend in the hair of a servant at the full moon.
Boil in the right eye of a sailor lost at sea,
This potion will surely make us laugh with glee.

>Controlling the future,
>Controlling the past
>Their minds are ours with
>This potion we cast.

Sieve the ashes of a commander of France
This will make them go into a trance.
The wings of a queen bee of a hive.
Blend with the tongue of a friend that's alive.

>Controlling the future,
>Controlling the past
>Their minds are ours with
>This potion we cast.

The two toes of the most powerful man
The brains of a loyal dog fried in a pan
Stir in a wig made from a horse's tail,
Dissolve in the mushrooms of a pixie's trail
This potion we make will never fail.

>Controlling the future,
>Controlling the past
>Their minds are ours with
>This potion we cast.

Lucy Buzzacott (13)
Meole Brace School

Jack And The Beanstalk Ballad

Chorus
Jack and his mum are desperately poor,
Their only belonging was a cow
Jack sells Daisy for some beans and no more,
What will his poor family do now?

Jack sold Daisy for some beans
He got them from a weird woman,
Never climb the beanstalk at the top there's something mean,
You will never find these in a can.

Chorus

There was a beanstalk in their backyard
It was huge, green and covered in beans,
Jack started to climb, it was very hard
As he climbed he ripped his jeans.

Chorus

At the top a castle stood,
There was a giant chanting a tune,
He smelt Jack's blood,
The giant was as tall as the moon.

Chorus

Jack ran away, the giant chased after
He had a brilliant plan,
He started to chop the beanstalk down,
The giant is a dead man.

Andrew Jones (12)
Meole Brace School

Jack And The Beanstalk

Jack, he bought the magic beans
His mother she began to cry
Planted beans gave the old man the means
To climb up into the sky.

Poor Jack he badly needs some food
So his mother won't be in a mood
He sold his donkey that was mean
And then he got some magic beans.

Jack, he bought the magic beans
His mother she began to cry
Planted beans gave the old man the means
To climb up into the sky.

He showed his mum, she said it was no good
And she wanted a really good pud
But they were magic, she didn't know
Then she chucked them out the window.

Jack, he bought the magic beans
His mother she began to cry
Planted beans gave the old man the means
To climb up into the sky.

He went to bed tired and hungry
In the morning it was dark outside
For the bean had grown into a tree
And then his heart was filled with pride.

Jack, he bought the magic beans
His mother she began to cry
Planted beans gave the old man the means
To climb up into the sky.

The giant got hungry and looked around
And started to eat Jack from the ground.

Laura Roberts (12)
Meole Brace School

Genius Potion

Into this potion we shall add
The hair from a scientist - must be mad,
Add the largest calculator
Mashed up brains of legislator
Knowledge of one thousand people
Rats from a forgotten steeple.

Chorus
Now stir this mixture three times through
Until it becomes as thick as goo

Add the skin of a teacher's lips
Into the cauldron, fry and mix
Strip an owl of a feather
Sun or rain, whatever weather,
A dictionary from a school,
This potion is a crafty tool.

Chorus

Remains of orphaned baby brains
Every part of a whiz kid's veins
A spoonful of correct answers,
Feet of several ballet dancers
Omega 3 from oily fish
This will give you a brainy dish.

Blend in guts of a musician
You'll go on an expedition
Spice it up with bits of sage
This will work whatever your age.

Chorus
Now stir this mixture three times through
Until it becomes as thick as goo

A professor from a college
This brew is a font of knowledge.

Kirsten Jones (13)
Meole Brace School

Potion For Power

Come round the cauldron, flower,
You, we'll make king and power.

In it throw gold of crown,
Add heir with flowing gown.
Mash politician's mind,
With posh voice we will bind
You in expensive clothes
'Tis 'nough to make you loath.

Chorus

Wheel of limousine
Hands of driver are mean.
Give you Union Jack,
Queen bees sting from the back,
Weapons of bodyguards.
Mansion door is too hard,
But steam it up we shall,
Make it soft as your pal.

Chorus

Chop up lots of money,
Mash brain that's so smarty,
Mix in some dragon's heart,
Then power will be art.

Chorus

Eat up some chunky warm bread,
Have a good night in your bed
Drink up this potion, all up,
You'll have power by sun up.

Tom Burke (13)
Meole Brace School

Invisibility Serum

Gather round, gather round,
Stir well it must be brown.

In it throw an eye of newt
In it pour a pint of dew,
Add to it a taste of bad
This enough to make you mad.

Chorus

Throw in parrot it is cute
Add a scrap of pure, cold pewter
One glass of distilled water
Entrails of a recent slaughter.

Chorus

Mash up poisoned tongue of sprite
Stir in colour make it white,
Add the scent of stinky poo
Now I shall add something new.

Chorus

Chameleon's tainted heart
Wheel of a wooden cart,
Decayed, preferably must
If not, potion will go bust.

Gather round, gather round
Stir well it must be brown.

James Robinson (13)
Meole Brace School

Potion Of Flight

In with a wing of an eagle
Sickly, deadly and illegal
Mixed around inside my pot
A fairy cake this is not
A brain of a pilot set for the air
Foot of a budgie straight from its lair.

Churning, churning all around
My feet are up and off the ground.

Silky feathers of a fairy
Head of a goblin that's still wary
Chopped up, bleeding fingernails
Enough to send you off the rails
Glowing strong my yellow eyes
Lift me up amongst the flies.

Chorus

Corpse of a pigeon I do add
Entrails crawling make me glad
For hours now I have stirred
To gain these powers of a bird
And now I see it in my mind
It's strange and of the weird kind
I see me jumping from a top
Soaring on no will to stop
Now I'm back in the land of the living
Bloody hands look unforgiving
These ingredients I will fry
Lift me up and make me fly.

Chorus

Will Andrews (13)
Meole Brace School

Invisibility Potion

Chorus
Boil and brew, all will be the key,
And something will be, that you cannot see.

The wings of three rats
Are richer than cats.
The legs of a snake,
Will boil and bake.
The scales of a plant,
Are mashed in this chant.
The tail of a sheep,
And crocs that can weep.
The voice of a bird,
That's never been heard.
The sniffles of turd,
And all that's been stirred.

Chorus

The ego of a bear,
One leg of a chair.
The age of a rose,
All these that I chose.
The eyes of an owl,
A shark and its bowl,
And blood that's been chilled,
And a heart that's been grilled.
A blue and red hole,
That's packed full with coal.
You'll know with your soul,
That the subject's not whole.

Chorus

Toby Kirk (14)
Meole Brace School

The Evil Potion!

This is a potion from Hell
It's so evil can't you tell
First simmer in a wolf's head
The brewer will soon be dead
Pupil of hyena's eyes
Stir it in with many lies.

Turn it, stir it, and make it boil
Down below the infirm soil.

Add snakes' venom to your broth
Churn it up and make it troth
Strength imposed with gators' teeth
Greasy slime, death lies beneath
Throw in a rancid rat's tail
My death potion cannot fail.

Turn it, stir it, and make it boil
Down below the infirm soil.

Wrap dead mice in wing of bat
Watch the cauldron hiss with fat
Maggots live in lizard's tongue
Into the pot they are slung
The cauldron boils to the brim
Victim's lives are looking grim.

Ricky Evans (13)
Meole Brace School

A Frog's Day

Jumping!
Coming nearer
Splashing all around me.
Suddenly, quiet, he's jumped away
Leap frog!

Molly Derbyshire (11)
Meole Brace School

To Make A Potion For Eternal Life And Youth

For a drink fit for Heaven
You must make this in Devon
First add feather of phoenix,
Then the centre of a helix
Hair of elf, elephant's tusk
Drink this potion, it's a must!

Jump from cloud to cloud above
Fly high like a soaring dove.

Stir in the page of a book
Leave it for a while, let it cook.
Ashes from a cremation
The guilt from a confession
Let it steam, then add diamonds
Earth from a hill in Holland
Lastly add a bit of trust
Drink this potion, it's a must!

Jump from cloud to cloud above
Fly high like a soaring dove.

Now the potion works a treat
Give it to all that you meet.

Peter Kilby (13)
Meole Brace School

Wolves

I love
Wolves; I don't
Know why people hate them.
They are beautiful, amazing
And free.

Annabelle Bowyer (13)
Meole Brace School

Invisibility Potion

Dice the ingredients of this potion
For this invisibility lotion,
Slip quietly through places never seen
You will find no trace of where you have been.

Magic is tragic if you cannot see,
This can conjure invisibility.

Add slime of a slug to chameleon's tail
Throw in the sweet song of a nightingale
Pop in the bubbles brewed fresh from water
In goes the dog's eye straight from the slaughter.

Chorus
Finishing touches, a single moth's wing
Snakes' skin and sunlight, which ghost essence brings,
Now you can drink up your complete potion
Go anywhere, using any motion.

Magic is tragic if you cannot see,
This can conjure invisibility.

Alex Roberts (13)
Meole Brace School

My False Desire

It was like when you have been searching all night
(I am stuck, I am stuck, I am stuck) and then it hit.
Hit hard, and I realised that all this time it had been with me.

It had been in me, like a red blood cell
Acting like a part of me; my desire had been with me all along.

I was twisted within myself,
I didn't want to act.

Douglas Tenison-Collins (11)
Meole Brace School

Love Charm

From him 3 drops of deep coloured blood
Collected in a dark and dingy wood
3 oysters boiled in the shells
To symbolise our future, wedding bells.

Forget-me-not petals I need to stew
To represent each year I have loved you

Murder the soul of a love filled dove
From me 3 drops of blood packed with love
Snatch from an innocent swan, their heart
From him I wish to never ever part.

Forget-me-not petals I need to stew
To represent each year I have loved you

A lock of his chocolate-coloured hair
After this charm we shall become a pair
Of intoxicating wine, 3 drops
This charm will make my rival's heart go pop!

Forget-me-not petals I need to stew
To represent each year I have loved you

Forget-me-not petals I need to stew
To represent each year I have loved you.

Lucy Baker (14)
Meole Brace School

Watch The Flow Of Art
(A cinquain)

The art,
Watch the pencil,
Drawing, colouring, feel
The way the paintbrush flows, dances
And stops.

Rachel Austin (11)
Meole Brace School

Shut Up Potion

Firstly take the person,
Whose mouth you want to shut.
Then take a hair from their head,
And mix the potion up.

Chorus
Simmer, stir, boil and bake,
For the frozen tongue
This potion make.

Cauldron next needs the whisker
Of the mouse that's quiet and shy
Whisk the whisker in a whisk
Then put in the pot to fry.

Chorus

Now we need from an owl,
A feather that's soft and white.
And we'll also need the silence
Of the illuminated night.

Chorus

Three legs of a spider
The shadow of a cloud
And don't forget the tongue
Of the frog that's no longer loud.

Chorus

The petals of a daisy
For the final touch
The whisper of the winter wind
We don't need very much.

Chorus

Harriet Cockill (14)
Meole Brace School

Knowledge Potion

In this cauldron we must brew
Things that will ensure us to
Become so very clever,
That we will be forever
So knowledgeable that we
Will know for eternity.

Chorus
Stir it round and heat it up,
Pour it in the golden cup,
Drink it now and make it,
So we shall never be thick.

Drop in eye of an eagle,
We will make our dreams legal
Next goes in an owl's head,
Pillows from a dead man's bed,
The core root from an oak tree,
We'll know for eternity.

Chorus

Next boil and add the page
Of a good book, crisp and beige,
Then the shell of a tortoise
And the fin of a porpoise,
Stir it round then let it be
We'll know for eternity.

Chorus

Alice Windows (13)
Meole Brace School

Revenge

Ray of sunshine from the sky,
All bad thoughts can say goodbye
Hand from clock, last struck twelve,
Into a poet we must delve,
To reach his still beating heart
Now let the happiness start.

Magic will get nice and hot,
In my multicoloured pot.

Steal the music from the world
Add the vomit of child just hurled,
Pinch of salt will make it true,
Stir in happiness from you,
And now you'll know how it feels,
Keep it safe in skin of seals.

Magic will get nice and hot,
In my multicoloured pot.

Now this spell is almost through
And you will feel this curse too
Wing of innocent magpie
And now you'll pay for your lie,
Lastly a tear, from my heart
Now it is time, let it start!

Laura Gwilliams (14)
Meole Brace School

Chickens

(A cinquain)

Chickens
Cuddly funny
So warm with feather coats
Head bobbing up and down with glee.
Chickens.

Elliot Townsend (11)
Meole Brace School

Potion For Speed

Stir for speed, mix to make,
I need a potion to eat with my cake.
A lick of Lucozade, a cheetah's leg
You will run like the wind and slither like a snake,
1 tattered trainer and 2 broken boots,
Then you can add the dandelion roots.

Stir for speed, mix to make
I need a potion to eat with my cake,
Magazine cut-outs from Four Four Two
A spoonful of sugar or maybe a few,
5 little toes from Ian Thorpe's feet
And 5kg of dead spirits' meat.

Stir for speed, mix to make,
I need a potion to eat with my cake.
Just 1 more ingredient, this is the one,
That will make you go fast
Before the clock strikes 1
Just a single . . . drop . . . of human . . . *blood!*

Rebecca Ellis (14)
Meole Brace School

Shopping!

(A cinquain)

Shopping
Is exciting,
So very, very fun.
It is enjoyed by everyone . . .
It's fun!

Ruth Lunt (11)
Meole Brace School

The Nightmare

It is when you have been
Searching all night
When you have been
In such a fright
I am stuck!
I am stuck!
There was nothing in sight.

I run as fast as I can
I am stuck!
I am stuck!
I see this man,
A scary face
I am stuck!
I am stuck!

The trees reached up
Each branch twisted round
Then I fell to the ground
I am stuck!
I am stuck!
I woke up and it was a dream
No it doesn't seem
I tried to remember where I had been.

Natalie Robson (11)
Meole Brace School

Football!

(A cinquain)

I like
Football, because
It is the best sport in
The world. I'm passionate about
Football!

Robert Carey (11)
Meole Brace School

The Noise

Everything is quiet, all around.
Everything is quiet, even on the ground
Then all of a sudden, a shuffling noise
Is it a bunch of naughty boys?

Rustling, sneaking, as slowly as can be.
If I get closer, maybe I can see
Not too close, I might scare it away
It's getting dark, the clouds are grey.

What could it be? I don't have a clue
It looks quite small; I don't know what to do
I think it's red, or maybe brown
It looks at me and gives a frown.

It's shuffling slowly, nearer to me
My body's shaking, as well as my knee
Is it a rabbit, or a small fox?
I'm so scared I fiddle with my locks.

As it approaches me very, very slowly
It looks at me, as if it knows me.
From where I am, I can now see.
That it's a squirrel, looking at me.

Robert Clayton (13)
Meole Brace School

Chocolate

(A cinquain)

Yummy
I love it so
Brown and yummy, nice too
Galaxy, Mars, Smarties, Snickers
Scrummy.

Jessica Marsden (11)
Meole Brace School

I Need To Sleep!

It was like when you have been searching all night
I always feel like that.
I wake up in the morning and feel really tired.
It may be better if I was an actor and this went
                        when the curtains closed.

I'm feeling really blue.
I feel so very tired,
I must have been awake all night
But I must have forgotten,
I just feel like going back to bed, but I know I can't.
My eyes keep closing, but then they decide to open again.

My brain feels so twisted
I need to *sleep!*

Amy Lewis (11)
Meole Brace School

The Bookely

It was like when you have been searching all night,
For something you've lost,
But different.
There was a Bookely under my bed one night.

The Bookely's body was orange,
With purple and green spots.

I recognised the Bookely from the theatre.
I am stuck! I am stuck, in a world of confusion
When will this riddle be solved?
My mind has been twisted!
I am stuck, I am stuck, I am stu . . .

Lauren Gwilt (12)
Meole Brace School

It Was There

It was like when you have been searching all night.

You were stuck, lost maybe
You just couldn't find that precious item
I'm stuck, I'm stuck, and I'm stuck!
It seemed I had lost it forever.

I'm stuck, I'm stuck, and I'm stuck!
My face was red - I was so tired
I'm stuck, I'm stuck, and I'm stuck.
My head was clapping
My brain was hurting -
I couldn't find it anywhere.

I'm stuck - I'm stuck
I'm stuck - I'm stuck
Suddenly my head twisted round,

It was there, staring back at me.
I had found it.
It was there!

Kathryn Donnelly (11)
Meole Brace School

Contradictions

'In my eyes you are more lovely than life'
This man could later be an assassin
Threatening lives, he could live with a knife.
Maybe a lady's heart he wants to win.
A man who has killed millions in war,
A man who has fought bravely - dropped a bomb;
Could, if he returned, step in his front door,
Pat his dog and his troubles would be gone.
For some have done things that are saddening,
And all have done things that are so gladdening,
So do not object when somebody hates;
Think of what you've done, before it's too late.

Phoebe Ruxton (12)
Meole Brace School

Darkness

It was like when you have been,
Searching all night.
In the cold,
And the dark,
But nothing can be found.
Black and empty.
Swirling into nowhere
But nothing but black,
Can be seen.

I stared and I stared
As looking into space
Staring into nothing,
But looking for something.

The darkness twisted,
In front of my eyes
Swirling,
And spinning.
Spinning and spinning,
Towards me.

I opened my eyes!

Anthony Smith (13)
Meole Brace School

Swimming
(A cinquain)

Swimming
It's stroke for stroke,
It is fast and gruelling
Breaststroke, front crawl, backstroke is best
Water.

Hazel Tetsill (12)
Meole Brace School

I'm Stuck . . .

It was like when you have been searching all night . . .
I am stuck, I am stuck,
I am stuck, I am stuck,
I am stuck, I am stuck . . .
My favourite colour is purple,
My least favourite colour is grey.

I'm stuck, I'm stuck,
My pen is pink with
A white love heart on it.
My friend is Charlie.
I am in English.
My teacher is Ms Bolmer.
I like theatres
And going to watch them.

I like drinking water.
I am stuck, I am stuck.
I hate going on rides
That are twisted.
I hate roller coasters.
I am stuck, I am stuck . . .
I love doing art and drama
Boo! 'Miaow!'
I am stuck, I am stuck,
I am stuck.

Vicky Taylor (13)
Meole Brace School

Cricket

(A cinquain)

Cricket
Bat and wickets
Balls flying fast at me
Smack, my bat swings: that's a good shot
Cricket.

Stephen Barnard (12)
Meole Brace School

Witches

It was like when you had been searching all night,
Trees pressed in all around,
Their leafage as dark as the night sky,
I am stuck,
I am stuck.

I am walking,
It was like I had no sense of direction,
I am stuck,
I am stuck.

I could hear voices,
'She's over there.'
'Oh no she isn't.'
'Oh yes she is.'
I am stuck,
I am stuck.

Then I came to a clearing,
A lady tied to a flaming post,
Screaming,
While flames licked around her feet,
She is stuck,
She is stuck.
Another life lost, I thought as flames twisted round her.

Michael L'argent (13)
Meole Brace School

Pizza

(A cinquain)

I like
Pizza! It's great!
I eat it every day
Toppings of pineapples and ham
Yum-yum!

James Carter (11)
Meole Brace School

What Was It?

I thought it was
a frog
but it was only
moss on the ground
half covered by the grass.

I thought it was
a bee
but it was only
a leaf
blowing in the wind.

I thought it was
a spider
but it was only
a fly
on the wall.

I thought it was
a mummy
but it was only
a doll covered in bandages
for my sister's project
lying on the floor
half covered with clothes.

Jamie Holden (12)
Meole Brace School

My World!
(A cinquain)

My world
A super place;
People all around me;
My mum, dad, brother and sister.
My life.

Alice Bowen (13)
Meole Brace School

Christmas

Christmas is a time of fun and joy,
Stockings, presents and many a toy,
Little children trying to sleep in their beds
A thought of presents and gifts running through their heads.

Out come the decorations once more
Lights, trees and a wreath on the door.
Everything's quiet, it's Christmas night
Only Santa is heard, what a magical sight.

But if you listen closely, you may hear someone crying
Because for some, they do not receive
No lights, trees, but they only grieve.
Children are in pain, their hearts slowly dying.

You may be happy, but share a thought
For those in pain and who are distraught.

Anneka Gorman (14)
Meole Brace School

Led Zeppelin

I love the band Led Zeppelin
They changed the world of rock.
Their music is much better,
Than today's hip-hop and pop.

Jimmy Page is my favourite
But they're all pretty good,
My dad saw them in concert
I only wish I could.

Now I'll never see them in action;
Their drummer is long dead.
You can never replace a band member,
It's like having a hole in the head.

Matt Clough (13)
Meole Brace School

Christmas!

People singing happy and jolly,
The festival season of mistletoe and holly,
Building snowmen and snowball fights,
Burning fires and bright yellow lights.

Families gather for the fun,
Eating pies and lots of buns,
Sleepy children rush down to the tree,
Open presents with a smile of glee.

Roaring through the presents one by one,
The smiles disappear; eventually they're gone,
They rush outside nothing but bare,
No snow to be seen or white anywhere,

Christmas is over, they rush inside,
To gather round the fire and look outside.

Sian O'Hanlon (13)
Meole Brace School

Weather

Nobody knows what the weather will bring,
Rain, snow, hail, please sunshine, please sunshine,
Sunshine is what many of us will sing,
Snow, sun, please rain, please rain, others will whine.
    No one can rule the weather to our dreams,
    So why do we complain? Why do we groan?
    We always want it our way so it seems,
    We shouldn't waste breath on the constant drone.
Summer's gone and it hasn't been great,
Hopefully next year it will have improved,
It could be wet which most of us will hate.
So don't moan, our summers cannot be moved.
    Always enjoy the good weather we get,
    If it's bad please don't moan or get upset.

Sebastian Salamat (12)
Meole Brace School

Night Drama

It was like when you have
Been searching all night
When you finally find it
It could give you a fright.

    The night was dark
    The stars were bright
    Shining white
    Extremely bright.

        The breeze was freezing cold
        Like a sharp, Atlantic wind
        The performance of the shooting stars
        Went on from Earth to Mars.

It was very strange
The feeling about
A shadow face stared
Sort of mysterious it was
Mysterious, cold and twisted.

Ellen Brenner (12)
Meole Brace School

Aussie Beasts

When I went to Australia I saw;
A koala snoozing,
A kangaroo jumping,
A kookaburra singing
A platypus swimming,
A dingo growling,
And a wombat snoring,
That is what I saw.
I saw these Aussie beasts!

Becky Lloyd (13)
Meole Brace School

The Thing

I thought it was
A bat
But it was only
My black T-shirt flapping away on the line.

I thought it was
An elephant
But it was only
A grey truck
Driving through.

I thought it was
A crocodile
But it was only
A moss-covered log
Floating down the Severn.

I thought it was
A tortoise
But it was only
A rock with leaves over it
Sticking out of the ground.

Bassam Khalaileh (12)
Meole Brace School

The Search

It was like when you have been searching all night,
When you can't find something but you really need it,
Your mind is black and empty trying to remember where you put it,
It seems as though you have searched a whole theatre,
But you still can't find it.
Then you think you remember where you put it,
But you find that it is not what you want.

Josh Meredith (13)
Meole Brace School

It Looked Like . . .

I thought it was a fish
But it was only black leather
Frozen
In the ice.

I thought it was a snake
But it was only a big, long, green sock
Which had fallen off the washing line
Next door.

I thought it was a polar bear
But it was only a snowball
That I made last night
Rolling towards me.

I thought it was a monster
But it was only a boy
Going trick or treating
On Hallowe'en.

I thought it was a water fountain
But it was only an illusion
In a boiling hot desert.

Alex Cartwright (12)
Meole Brace School

Monkeys!

(A cinquain)

Monkeys
Monkeys are cool
Monkeys are really cute
Monkeys are the best and I love
Monkeys!

Melissa Thorpe (13)
Meole Brace School

It Was Only . . .

I thought it was
a robin
but it was only
a bunch of leaves
half buried in twigs and berries.

I thought it was
a crocodile
but it was only
a stump of wood
in the shape of a crocodile.

I thought it was
a bogeyman
but it was only
a tree in the wind
moving in the black night.

I thought it was
a tiger
but it was only
plants and planks of wood
half buried in grass and sawdust.

Jessica Gale (12)
Meole Brace School

Poem About School

S chool.
C lasses to go to.
H omework to be done.
O pen your bag, get ready for class.
O pen your book, do some work.
L earning new things every day.

Daniel Morris (13)
Meole Brace School

What Was It?

I thought it was
A ladybird
But it was only
A person wearing
A red and black T-shirt
Walking to work.

I thought it was
A bee
But it was only
My mobile alarm going off.

I thought it was
A snake
But it was only
The grass brushing
My leg.

I thought it was
A spider
But it was only a hairy log.

I thought it was
A cow
But it was only my sister
A cow in the pantomime.

Pippa Cox (13)
Meole Brace School

Love

(A cinquain)

In love
My mind goes blank
My lips go dry, I flush -
How can I express my feelings?
Love struck.

Dannielle Natasha Tennant (13)
Meole Brace School

Five Minutes

Five minutes to go,
I've got to pop to the shop,
To get some soap for the mop.

Four minutes to go,
I'm back from the shop,
With my soap for the mop.

Three minutes to go,
Got to go back to the shop,
For some extremely fizzy pop.

Two minutes to go,
I'm back from the shop,
With my extremely fizzy pop.

One minute to go,
No time to go back to the shop,
Jobs to be done with a skip and hop.

No minutes to go,
It's finally time to stop,
What was the rush? What was the hurry?
I think I've lost the plot!

Kate Brett (12)
Meole Brace School

Haiku

The cold, frosty morn,
The ground as hard as a brick,
With the trees lifeless.

Hannah Mainwaring (12)
Meole Brace School

Woodland Walk

Beneath the dappled shade of trees,
Earthy smells reach out to caress,
Autumn leaves gently quiver,
With every breath of wind.

A fiery carpet of golden keys,
Cover the ground,
Hiding the tracks of the forest people,
Who hide away in secret places.

Lichen and moss hold fast,
To rocky ledges,
Whilst water drips,
Drips from their damp bodies.

Long fingers reach down,
From the high boughs of the wood giants,
Their once fine green hair,
Has turned to fawn and amber.

Nuts turn ripe,
With the coming of autumn,
And squirrels collect their bounty,
Before dashing up nearby trees to safety,

And when the leaves have all fallen,
And the ground is burning apricot,
The smell of wood smoke will fill the air,
And an autumn sun will set.

Gemma Cusack (13)
Meole Brace School

The Harbour

(A haiku)

The harbour was calm
Then the rattling of the machine guns
And death filled the air.

Sam Whittaker (12)
Meole Brace School

Hunting!

Fight the ban! Fight the ban!
They all shout and cheer,
Not for once thinking,
For the little fox's fear,
And he does feature,
In hunting, poor creature.

Victim of the hounds,
He runs for all he's worth,
They are in hot pursuit,
Followed by the Devil dressed in red,
White breeches, blood-stained,
Clasping the horn, ready for the kill,
Cloven feet hidden in polished riding boots.

The horn sounds,
The fox's heart pounds,
Where shall I go?
But it's too late.
He is torn up and half ate.
Now ask yourself,
Is this a sport?

So, all you hunting folk out there,
What you're doing is *not* fair,
Foxes don't know what they eat isn't right,
Which proves hunting is harsh and light.

Ebony May Pharo (13)
Meole Brace School

The Waterfall
(A haiku)

Flowing water, crash
Hitting the sharp rocks below
Blue, cold waters slide.

Caldy Walton (12)
Meole Brace School

Number 6

Number 6 Lime Lane is no ordinary place,
Jam-packed, bursting at the seams.

Running up the stairs, the running of water, the dog barking.

'Where's my hairbrush?'
'Mum!'
'Can't find my sock, bag, anything!'
'You can't just have that for breakfast.'
'We're late.'
'Drink up.'
'Let's go!'

Off to school.
The car starts!
Forgotten lunch.
Open the door.
Off to school.
Lime Lane is quiet, well not quite: the dog's still barking.

Back home to number 6.
No, this time it isn't the dog.
Baby banging saucepans.
The oldest shouting, 'Stop it!'
Sisssss from the saucepan overflowing.
All fed.
All quiet.

The lights are out at number 6
And the rest of Lime Lane can enjoy peace - until morning.

Ellen Alexander (11)
Meole Brace School

Butterfly

Ugly transforms to
Beauty that waltzes with air
Maybe things can change . . .

Danielle Haywood (13)
Meole Brace School

The Wiggle

The wiggle is a murderous thing,
With gleaming eye and sweeping wing,
With talons sharp and beak so hard,
I'm sure it lives in my backyard.
In a high-up nest of twigs and mud,
Lined with putrid field mouse blood,
And in that nest lie fearful chicks,
That sit all day like builder's bricks.
They screech and howl and wail for food;
They put me in an awful mood.
I'm frightened just because I know,
That it will try to get me so -
At night-time while I lie awake,
It scrapes the window, makes it quake.
It tries to reach the prey inside,
The other night I nearly cried -
It scraped and nearly broke the pane,
And nearly let in all the rain.
But thankfully it flew away,
To sit in its nest all night and day,
And watch for something to devour,
To pick at bones hour after hour.
Who will the next victim be?
I'll sit inside and wait and see.
Who'll be next? I've not a clue -
A dog? A cat? Or maybe . . .
You!

Charlotte Lewis (11)
Meole Brace School

Butterflies

Blessed with paired wings,
And a delicate nature,
Lies the butterfly.

Annie Lam (12)
Meole Brace School

Lost
(A sonnet)

Why do I wander these old days alone?
No light through my window that I can see,
My life has gone, no place I can call home,
I have never seen love as love sees thee.
The pain hurts so much I cannot believe,
Now the days get harder as I go on.
Each breath that I take gets harder to breathe,
Miss you like the flower misses the sun.
I hope that your spirit goes to the sky,
Although now I am a lost wanderer,
But it is to live as it is to die,
I now know there is a land down yonder.
Now I am found although I still do grieve,
But life is so short we all have to leave.

Robert Wilson (13)
Meole Brace School

The River
(A haiku)

It starts as a spring,
Way up in the mountain top.
Will it ever end?

Susannah Williams (12)
Meole Brace School

Rising Sun

Rising sun:
Illuminating the sky,
And the morning comes.

Robert Edward Howarth Savage (12)
Meole Brace School

Isle Of Man

An island in the middle of the sea,
Its magical stories, full of folklore,
Back in time, a holiday full of glee,
A heaven for the rich, no joke for poor.
Horse trams on seafronts, take us back in time,
Three legs of man, the symbol of the isle,
Tynwald, the day of laws and deals with crime.
Wave at the Fairy Bridge and throw a smile.
The loss of the tail began at the ark.
The Vikings from old, the bike racing too.
'Fairies are not true' - don't make that remark!
To get there you need the ferry - *wooho!*
Say hi to the fairies or you won't get home.
The Manx cat roaming the isle, no tail!

Harriet Davies (12)
Meole Brace School

The Sunset
(A haiku)

The blue sea glistens,
With the soft, slow, gentle waves,
As the warm sun sets.

Callum Chatham (12)
Meole Brace School

Morning
(A haiku)

The sun is rising.
The animals get up from
Their tiny burrows.

Michael Abbott (12)
Meole Brace School

My First Day

Felt like I was born again,
My tie like a snake round my neck,
As cold as ice,
Shaking like jelly.

Hall as big as two great whales,
Year 11s towering over me like skyscrapers,
Got loose a couple of times,
Hoping I would make new friends,
I was scared like an elephant who saw a mouse,
My first lesson hard as rocket science.

Relieved I survived the first day,
Could not wait to come home,
Made lots of friends,
And learned where to go.

Brad Smith (11)
Meole Brace School

Full Moon
(A haiku)

Full moon bright and new,
Sparkling in a velvet sky,
Lighting up the night.

Callum Bebb (12)
Meole Brace School

Wanderer
(A haiku)

Late night wanderer
Plods down the unbeaten path
He wanders, wanders.

Aidan Lo (12)
Meole Brace School

What Was It?

I thought it was
a fish
but it was only
a piece of paper
getting tossed around by the wind.

I thought it was
a bat
but it was only
a black sock
stuck in a tree.

I thought it was
a ghost
but it was only
my white shirt
which had fallen
on the floor.

Amy Lewis (12)
Meole Brace School

My Drum Set

I have a set of drums,
that are situated in my home,
but when I hit the bass,
they look at me in such disgrace,
that the people make a funny face.

When I rattle my snare,
it makes most people stare.
The noise makes my mum and dad go spare.

I now crash the cymbal,
which is worse than the snare,
I hit the cymbal with so much care,
but just as fast as a hare.

Chris Duffy (12)
Meole Brace School

Sadness Without A Loved One!

Your sadness is like a flower,
Swaying in the blindingly bright, midnight sun,
Rising above the horizon,
Swaying so gently,
Swaying so free,
Swaying away in its own time.

It may be hard,
It may be sad,
But you have just got to remember,
The good times you've had together.

The way you laughed together,
The way you talked together,
But most of all,
You'll remember the love you had together,
The love that kept you together,
Always and forever.

Hayley Jenks (12)
Meole Brace School

My Euro 2004

It was amazing footie every day.
Sun shining down.
Big shocks on the way.
Great football, wonderful goals
But best of all me meeting Scholes.
First shock, France go out
And Greece in with a shout.
Next shock, England are cheated
Go home sad and defeated.
All this and still the first day.
Yes, this is going to be a good holiday.

Joe Streeter (12)
Meole Brace School

My First Day At School

I was scared like an antelope
Being chased by a tiger,
I wasn't hungry a bit,
My throat was as dry as a ventilation shaft.

In the hall at school,
My mind was racing like Kelly Holmes in the last 50 metres.
My first proper lesson, Maths,
Trying to think of answers.
But I was thinking about going home too much.
I felt trapped,
Like an animal in a zoo.

The end of the day,
I was tired.
When I got into the car I nearly fell asleep instantly
Like a baby.

Connor Marston (12)
Meole Brace School

My First Day

When I got up
I got my uniform on
My tummy was upside down
My sister immediately grabbed the camera
In my uniform I felt brand new
I smiled for the camera and said, 'Cheese!'
On the way I felt like I was rolling down a hill
In a dustbin with no brakes.

When I got there I was sitting in reception
With my tummy twirling like a wheel of fortune
Mr Kaye came and took my form
He made me feel really welcome
At first I thought I wouldn't like it
But everything started coming together
And now I feel good about it.

Roseanna Corsentino (11)
Meole Brace School

My First Day At School

Today is the day!
I just wanted to stay in bed.
I did not want to walk so far.
New surroundings, pupils, friends, enemies, teachers.
When I got to school my legs shook like jelly.

All the Year 7s got called to the hall.
Mr Kaye's voice was so loud.
We got put into our forms.
I liked my form and made lots of friends.
My first lesson was maths.
I hated maths.
After that we had art then history.

School ended and I then had to walk home again.
I really enjoyed my first day at school.
I couldn't wait for Tuesday to arrive.
I am in big school at last.

Jessica Mullineaux (11)
Meole Brace School

Summer Love

Like an angel, out of the sky you came,
Cleaning up all the clouds, the sadness and the rain.

You filled the sky with your dazzling rays,
Vanished the winter nights and brought the summer days.

Your beams shine down and make the flowers bloom,
From misery to joy, you took away the gloom.

Everything back, the colours, the life,
Lakes so clear, as shiny as a blade on a knife.

White roses, pink fuchsias, sunflowers tall,
For how long? Winter will be back to take it all.

Rachael Thomas (13)
Meole Brace School

Guinness

I open thy door and enter thy room
How have I missed thee? How did I cope?
I walk to thy stool through a murky gloom
Waiting too long, it's like hanging on rope.

She walks towards me, thy time is now here
I look at the choice, which one shall I choose?
Thou dark like thy night, inside me I cheer
I walk to thy table, you I won't lose.

Thy smooth, tempting kiss, thou art just like cream
Over halfway down your sweet, sleek figure
Please don't go now, thou art like a dream
Last time I look at you, beauty you are.

If only you were a woman, I wish
But you are a stout beer, brewed by Irish.

David Payne (12)
Meole Brace School

Fairy Secrets

To shop, to school, to work and play,
The busy people pass all day,
They hurry, hurry, to and fro,
And hardly notice as they go,
The riverside flowers known so well,
Whose names so few of them can tell.

They never think of fairy folk
Who may be hiding for a joke.

If these people understood,
What's to be found by field and wood;
What fairy secrets are made plain,
By any footpath, road or lane,
They'd go with open eyes and look.

And then at least they'd learn to see,
How pretty obvious things can be.

Jessica Beardmore (13)
Meole Brace School

On My First Day

Today was the day
My knees were shaking like jelly
My breakfast was dry like sawdust
My car was like a big black panther
I did not want to get in it.

The school was like a big monster waiting to eat me
Mr Kaye's voice boomed like he had a megaphone
What would my teacher be like?
Would she be nice, strict, bossy?
I was with my best friend but I felt as if I was on another planet.

At lunch, what if I didn't have enough money?
Would I have to put everything back and starve?
What if the bell went and I was still eating?
Would I be late and get a detention?

At home time my mum asked me how it went
I said I'd made some new friends
So really it went great!

Millie Goodman (11)
Meole Brace School

School

S amantha shouts, 'We rock!'
C harlie throws a paper plane.
H arry knocks over a stack of books.
O livia pushes Harold over.
O llie scribbles on the chalk board.
L ucy breaks all the pencils.

What a commotion!
I wonder what the teacher will say?

Amy Fletcher (11)
Meole Brace School

My First Day

I thought I was going to get flattened
Like a little ant
But I woke up
I said it was just a dream
I faked a cold
'No, Aidan, get dressed,' they said.

That tie, it's choking me like snake
The shirt so itchy like ants all over me.

I barely got to school
But I looked so so cool
Bumped into a prefect
He said, 'Move, short stuff!'
But I was ok
I know I'm short
I was a bit hurt by him saying that
My first lesson was Maths, I hate Maths
The bell rang, I ran to the bus and got on safely
I got home from school
I said to my mum, 'School was ok
But I got lots of . . . *homework!*'

Aidan Wilkes (11)
Meole Brace School

Concentration

We ran blindly through selfish smoke
Germans snapping at our heels like dogs
Our eyes stung with tears and ash.

We sat rigidly in cramped trucks
Innocence pumping through our veins
Smelling fear on our neighbour.

We stood limply in dark-haired lines
The stars on our chests
Burning with one point too many.

Lucy Shaddock (13)
Meole Brace School

Innocent

Tonight's dinner swims quickly,
darting from side to side.
A Flicker of bright colours,
finding somewhere just to hide.

Up and down, past rocks,
round corals, shells and weed.
The sparkling surface shines,
a tasty, crunchy feed.

Up, up, up and away,
then down again like kites.
Swimming through an ocean,
an ocean full of frights.

And suddenly it's on you,
crashing like a wave.
But then it is silent,
silent as the grave.

The rumble of an engine,
there's danger all around.
A shadow in the sky,
a petrifying sound.

Soon it comes creeping,
as sly as a snake.
It may not mean to do this,
but your life it will take.

Like jaws enclosing you inside,
the end is not quite yet.
The innocent have done no wrong,
a dolphin in a net.

Sarah Lawrence (13)
Meole Brace School

My First Day At Meole Brace

Morning comes
It is time to get up
Looking at the mirror
Thinking what my day will be like
Staring up and down
Looking at my new uniform
My top button feels funny
I look older than before.

Spilling my drink all over the table
Teeth shaking nervously
The clock ticking to half-eight
Running up and down the stairs
Fetching and making sure
I've got all my books.

Soon as I know it
I'm walking to school with my friends
Wishing I could turn back
In the hall now
The head teacher's voice
Booming in my ears
Then dismissing us
From the hall.

Classroom; lost, big, scared, worried
All the Year 11s
Staring like big giants
Beaming down
Sitting by new people
Scared what they're going to be like . . .

Tineka Frost (11)
Meole Brace School

My First Day

Excited like a fly buzzing
With a weird feeling in my stomach.
My tie strangling me like a snake,
Feeling like someone else,
Stomach feeling like jelly.

Looking round to find my friends,
As Mr Kaye stood up with his voice booming
Like a full blast radio.
Mr Tillmans looked as tall as a giraffe.

First lesson maths.
Worried about what my teacher was going to be like.
The school was huge,
Nearly as big as the Eiffel Tower.

The end of the day,
Relieved I've done my first day.
Missed the school bus,
Can't believe it
So walked back with Anna,
A very good friend.

Francesca Huffa (12)
Meole Brace School

Hunger

There once was a loaf of bread,
That went by the name of Fred.
It smelt so nice,
It could have attracted mice
But then at least someone would have got fed!

Chris Sturge (13)
Meole Brace School

My Memory

As jolly as a sunny day.
As giggly as a hyena.
As wobbly as jelly.
As warm as cinders.
As sick as sea legs.

As suspicious as a guard.
As happy as a slug in the rain.
As wet as water.
As shocked as lightning.
As loud as a hi-fi.
As dark as the night.

As relieved as an escaped prisoner.
As high as a mountain.
As wobbly as jelly.
As giggly as a hyena.
As jolly as a sunny day.

Sam Noakes (11)
Meole Brace School

What Is The Moon?

The magical moon comes out at night
Silently creeping through the sky
Accompanied by the stars so bright
Gleams like a beacon up so high.

A glistening light shining down
The white ball fades away
The bright yellow sun steals the crown
As night turns into day.

Natalia Kirby (12)
Meole Brace School

My First Day At School

Hyper with excitement
But scared like a child in the dark
Rushing my breakfast
Got up very early
Putting on my new uniform
My tie gagging me like a snake around my neck
And top button horrible
Dancing around my house
Pictures being taken by friends and family
My legs like jelly
Eyes hurting from the flashes of the cameras.

Got into school
Shocked at how big it was
Got into the hall
Waiting, waiting for my form tutor
Then *yippee!* All my friends were in my form
Scared of getting lost
All my lessons were great
At the end of the day I loved it.

Charlotte Jones (11)
Meole Brace School

Deep In The Wood

Deep in the wood the creatures crawl.
What is it?
They scurry, scamper and sway,
As the night fades the day,
Like a candle's just been lit.

Deep in the wood the trees blow.
They moan and groan.
Swerving round and round.
What's that? I heard a sound.
The candle's just been blown.

Jean Hughes (11)
Meole Brace School

My First Day At Meole Brace

I was so scared I was shaking like jelly,
I woke up really early and I couldn't get to sleep the night before,
I was like an owl in the night,
I wouldn't go to sleep.

When I got to school we went to the hall,
I was as scared as a scaredy-cat,
I didn't know how to get around the school.

Then the bell rang which signified the start of the first lesson,
It was maths, I was really confident,
I got on with my maths teacher like a moth with light.

The day flew by, it was the end of the day already,
I was really relieved,
I had made lots of new friends
But it was as if I had known them for the whole of my life.

Kris Jackson (11)
Meole Brace School

My Trampoline!

As I was jumping through the air,
My neighbours would always stand and stare,
I would always think, *what a weird pair*,
But I always carried on without a care.
Then eventually came along Claire,
Who always sat in that same old chair,
So I stared at her with despair.
We were then just talking about my hair,
When I saw a big, fat, creamy éclair,
Which was very tempting if you're not aware,
So I tried to carry on without a care,
But then I thought of a horrid nightmare,
Which sent me flying into Claire,
So why didn't I just play my game of Solitaire?

Lily Cribbin (13)
Meole Brace School

Uncontrollable

Heart thumping, heat rising,
Lights flashing, smoke fuming,
Laughing, screaming, jumping, shouting,
Like a drug.

Heads slamming, shoulders rolling,
Hips banging, feet tapping,
Grinding, holding, bending, grabbing,
Can't stop.

Faces merging, floor bouncing,
Eyes glancing, skin tingling,
Flirting, singing, touching, impelling,
Uncontrollable.

Hair flinging, figures flickering,
Music beating, sad thoughts freeing,
Raving, provoking, affecting, enticing,
Everlasting.

Poppy Olah (13)
Meole Brace School

Sheep

Shall I compare thee to soft cotton wool?
Thou art more lovely and more soft
Thou will'st be sheared and the shops will'st be full
Thou will'st be fed by hay from the hay loft
To keep thee healthy, snug and warm
Thou will'st grow soft wool for the winter
Mr Tinter will look after the farm
A very nice man is Mr Tinter
When the spring comes thou will'st give birth
The newborn lamb will'st prance around
Soon the lamb will be hitting the earth
The cycle of a sheep goes round and round
    Shall I compare thee to soft cotton wool?
    Or shall I compare thee to wool on a spool?

James Bruce (12)
Meole Brace School

The Football Match

Hearts are racing,
Banging in their chests,
It's time to go,
Nerves are in shreds.

We step up to our positions,
Waiting for the whistle to blow,
Preparing, warming up,
Getting psyched up.

Having pep talks,
Mums and dads watching,
Friends waiting,
The atmosphere is silent, calm.

It is nearing the end,
Only ten seconds left,
She shoots, she scores -
Goal!

Nicola Thomas (11)
Meole Brace School

Liverpool FC

Shall I compare thee as angels on Earth?
Or shall I compare thee as giants that crush?
Liverpool won trophies on great English turf
With great players such as Souness and Rush
Liverpool now have Rafa to lead the charge
To gain former glory and win Premiership gold
This I feel is looming very large
And now we are playing like the Liverpool of old
Thou'rt now playing flash football with plenty of skill
And on the pitch thou is giving their all
And thou is playing with all their will
    With Stevie and Alonso at the heart of the team
    And now at long last thou will fulfil my great dream.

Matthew Hemstock (12)
Meole Brace School

Bullying

My head bent low towards the cold ground,
I'm blocking out everything, all of the sound.
People peering, jokers jeering, childish cheering.
Pummelling fists attack me,
Forcing me to the floor.
My life is like a soccer game, but I'm not allowed to score.
People peering, jokers jeering, childish cheering.
I didn't mean what I did that day.
I took the step of life,
Or I suppose you could call it death.
That van hit me like a hundred stabbing knives.
I loved you Mum,
I loved you Dad.
I won't be around anymore to make you feel sad.
I can't say in life that I really did try,
But now I finally must say goodbye.

Francine Hartshorn (13)
Meole Brace School

Eddie Stobart Poem

E very truck that goes down the road,
D elivers somewhere, but,
D efinitely the best company around,
I s,
E ddie Stobart Ltd!

S ome people have swanky lights,
T o draw people's attention,
O ther people have nameplates,
B ut not Eddie Stobart Ltd,
A ll Eddie's trucks,
R equire their own name,
T wiggy was the first!

L egend has it that Jools Holland,
T ravelling the motorways, started the,
D edicated Spotters Club!

Jacob Tiernan (11)
Meole Brace School

The Last Match Of The Season

As we stand in the crowd,
Taking a look at the ground that makes us proud,
Smelling the smell of just-cooked chips,
Hearing the joyful Telford fans chant.

But everything is not so happy anymore,
The last match of the season it is today,
But the thought through everyone's mind
What if this is the last ever?

Things have been a sorrowful blur,
Since that awful day,
'We've gone bankrupt,' we hear Andy Shaw say,
But even still we won't give up,
United forever, we'll keep fighting.

The whistle blows, the last match finished,
Fans run onto the pitch,
Desperately trying to get a last glimpse of the old squad,
Before it's too late.

The players come back out to say their last goodbyes,
To the club they have to leave behind.
The fans cheer and sing,
Trying to be positive, not knowing what the future might bring.

Eventually people start to leave,
Many in tears,
Saying goodbye to the team they've supported for years.
Saying goodbye to their friends in the stand,
See you next September - hopefully.

But now there is light at the end of the tunnel,
AFC Telford United, a newly-formed team,
I know one thing is true,
I'll always be Telford through and through.

Claire Jones (13)
Meole Brace School

Do You See Me?

Do you see the good underneath the mask?
You have a question, go on, ask.
Take a walk across a moonlit beach;
Look out at the water. Do you see me?
I'm here, I run wild, I run free;
I'm your enemy, I'm your friend.
What do you do to survive?
Is it that bad, a meal just to stay alive?
I can see you, I can smell you, where am I?
The tide's coming in, way up past your knees;
Rays of sunlight start to break, take a swim, please.
Beneath the steel-blue water lies a world;
My world, I'll show you, see me yet?
No you don't, I bet!
I'm stealthy; I'm like a fox only in water.
Getting louder is the steady drum of a motorboat.
I'm next to you, I'll have your throat;
I'm coming, I'll have you. No! No! I won't, not now.
Did I deserve this? Now you see me!
I'm no longer wild, no longer free;
Do you hear my cries? You swam in my water:
I was only trying to survive;
Now I'm no longer alive.
I'm now on show, next to dolphins and stingrays.
Now all I get is: 'Mummy, Mummy, look at the shark.'
The light in my life, gone, turned off, it's all gone dark.
I'm no longer invisible; I'm here for everyone to see.

Natasha Hall (13)
Meole Brace School

Passion

It lies in all of us
Ready to break out
Be unleashed boundless
Pure emotion, expression
The fire that fuels
Our most intense desires.

What is passion?
The death of Christ?
An act of passion?
An emotion that makes you impulsive?
A view you believe in?
Deep, intense feelings for something?
Is passion blind?

It's mostly unwanted
But we are all tainted
It can be the source
Of our finest moments
The ecstasy of love
The sorrow of grief
The clarity of hatred.

If we could live without passion
Maybe we'd know some kind of peace
But we would be hollow
Shuttered and dank
Empty rooms and empty space
Without passion we'd be truly *dead*.

Anna Davies (13)
Meole Brace School

Horses

He stands in the field, his head held high,
Prancing or dancing, bucking or rearing
Like he could reach the diamond-azure sky.
The end of a bright day, sunset nearing.

The sun dawning onto the winter's day,
A black and blue face filled the dying sky,
Hoping the winter sun will find a way.
Why the distant neighing? Why?

His silver mane sparkles in the moonlight,
His ruby-red nostrils, his jet-black eyes,
He takes flight through the coal-black, velvet night.

His breath danced on the early morning mist,
Green grass surrounded him. He was lonely
Like a small schoolboy waiting to be kissed.

Rosie Marsh (13)
Meole Brace School

Love

Thy eyes, as complex as the sky so far,
Hold beauty so divine, so exquisite.
Thy smile doest shine like a dazzling star,
The sun around thee dost seem to be lit.
Thou art my warrior, my handsome prince,
With the colour of gold upon thy fair head.
I've lov'd you since I met thee, and long since,
For thou art one whom for always I have car'd.
And as the church bells dost sing their deep chimes,
I think thou loves me, though I may be wrong.
Therefore like thee, my voice is held sometimes,
As I dare'st not bore thee with my song,
Before thou walk'st away through death's door,
Will thou be my loved one for evermore?

Jenny Hosty (12)
Meole Brace School

Birds

Thou fly freely whilst I stay on the ground,
Free from the first crack of internal life,
Why fly straight, when freedom permits flight round?
When freedom is thy spirit, 'tis no strife.

Man has tried for years, but thou fly with ease,
Flying machines, but none hath the God's gift,
The gift of flight, of which will never cease,
Delicate wing movement, lovely and swift.

Thy heart is pure, and commit anything selfish,
Indeed, they feed their children through the mouth,
For the sake of the birds, leave out the dish,
For the bird is extinct, north and south.

Though the bird has the title 'flying rat',
Though you spread no more disease than a cat.

Husnain Shah (12)
Meole Brace School

Tottenham Hotspur

Tottenham Hotspur are so skilful and great,
From Bill Nicholson to Robbie Keane,
When we think of Arsenal we're full of hate,
We're the best team ye world hath ever seen.
In 1961 we won the double,
With Blanchflower and manager Nicholson,
We won it easily, 'twas no trouble,
With goals from Smith and Terry Dyson.
In 1882 we were founded,
In 1901 we first won ye cup,
'Twas against one Sheffield United,
Since then seven more times we hath held 't up.
The league we won in '50 and '61,
Cup Winners Cup and much more we've also won.

Oliver Edwards (12)
Meole Brace School

Sky

The magical 'scape of the blue, blue sky,
The fluffy, white clouds' journey to Heaven,
Travelling slow as the day passes by,
And summer's reign in thy tranquil Britain.
When a sunny day turns to darkened night,
Angels look out of their little windows,
The tiny stars pierce the sky shining bright,
Waiting, waiting till the sun shows.
The bullets fall down upon the paved streets,
Rain, the angry, raging bull of the sky,
The miserable, sad cloud, a great, grey sheet,
Waiting for the anger to slowly die.
The flash of lightning, a gold phoenix call,
The furious roar from god of thunder,
Rain still pours on and darkness starts to fall,
Forked lightning shows this amazing wonder.
The magical 'scape of the blue, blue sky.
The beauty Mrs Rainbow, passes by.

Jessica Parry (13)
Meole Brace School

What I Feel

I feel like a song without the words.
A man without a soul.
A bird without its wings.
A heart without a hope.
I feel like a knight without a sword.
A sky without a sun.
You are the one that shines like the sun
Gleaming for everyone.
And I feel like a ship beneath the waves.
Nothing compared to you
Because you are the only one.

Nik Edwards (11)
Meole Brace School

Nature!

Blooming buttercups thou spread across fields,
Sheep nestled beautifully in thy sun,
Trees swaying gently in thy wind,
Thou shield the newly born bluebells dancing in fun.

Cows graze in thy grass, lambs chase the butterflies,
Hills in the distance are like soft, green bumps,
As the day goes on the view never dies,
In this magical world there are few dumps.

Nature is now such a wonderful place,
In every country you go to meet,
And even when you go out into space,
Nature will happily be there to greet.

The evening is coming, the night is near,
Not a cloud in the sky, the moon seems clear.

Rioja Gwynne-Porter (12)
Meole Brace School

Dizzy

Thou art as dark and velvety as night,
But thou hath paws that art of palest cream.
Thou hath eyes that shine star-like and bright,
When they art not closed whil'st in a dream.

When stalking a sparrow thy paws make no sound,
Once thou hath caught it thou just wants to play.
I am not happy when your presents are found,
So thou aren't fed for the rest of the day.

Peeking through the window I hear thy cry,
Guilty I feel for leaving thee outside,
Sunbathing in the garden thou doth lie,
Seeking attention rolling on thy side.

Thou looketh so cute and hard to resist,
But thou doesn't like to be hugged or kissed.

Louise Jones (12)
Meole Brace School

Autumn And Winter

Autumn leaves fall off the trees,
Red, yellow, brown,
They fall to the ground.

Dark nights are falling,
The owl is a-calling,
Autumn is here,
Fireworks will give cheer.

Jack Frost will appear,
A sign winter is here,
Snow falling,
Christmas Day is dawning.

We send out a cheer,
New Year is here!

Nathan Hinks (11)
Meole Brace School

Old Friend

There used to be someone in my life,
That made me smile, when things were bad,
And helped me wipe away the tears,
When I was sad.

That someone would always listen,
When no one else would.
And helped me find the answers
When no one else could.

That someone made me feel like I could fly,
I've been through some bad stuff,
But the worst was saying goodbye!

Katie Davies (13)
Meole Brace School

An African Sunrise

Rays of the golden sun creep over the dusty horizon,
A tide of blinding light ebbing gently over the savannah,
Tributaries of apricot, jade and terracotta,
Intertwine with the branches of a baobab tree.

Meerkats emerge from their tunnels in the crimson earth,
Nearby weaver bird architects design their intricate nests,
A hippo wades in a cool waterhole,
As a graceful impala drinks the refreshing water.

Herds of zebra gallop across the plains,
The sun changing their stripes from charcoal black
To a dull bronze,
A cacophony of cries fills the air.

A lion lies upon a warm rock,
His shaggy mane adorns his great head,
A magnificent plumage of brown, black and gold,
His hazel eyes widen with pride,
As he surveys the African sunrise.

Joseph Shaw (12)
Meole Brace School

Fire

Starts from a pretty spark,
Grows and grows,
Slowly starts to destroy,
A disaster is about to begin.

Getting bigger by the second,
Turning things to black, dark ash,
Lives could be taken,
Burning, boiling, smoky, death.
Fire!

Jacob Olah (11)
Meole Brace School

Through The Eyes Of A Spaceman

No shining light,
But stars so bright,
A little gleam,
No one can hear me scream,
Is this just a dream?

My spaceship battles on,
Battling for so long,
Through total darkness,
I'm such a mess,
Haven't even had time to rest.

There's meteors and asteroids,
Ain't no time for Polaroids,
To send back home to my kids and wife,
Could this be the end of my life?
Cut the atmosphere with a knife.

Zooming past all the planets,
No food, not even pomegranates,
No one knows what I mean,
Is this a real scene,
Or just somebody's TV screen?

Matt Galliers (13)
Meole Brace School

Ted And Fred

There once was a man called Ted,
He was best friends with Fred,
They lived together,
Happy as ever,
In an old, tumbledown shed.

Matthew Dodd (11)
Meole Brace School

The Forbidden

It was like when you had been searching all night
My legs were like jelly
My chest was aching
It felt like it was going to rip apart.

Then I saw it shiny and red
It just lay there all sparkly
It was beautiful
I couldn't see why it was forbidden.
As I moved closer I could see
It was striped like a tiger
I could see what seemed like curtains
Draped over it.

I stepped forward and picked it up
It was like a cold stone in my hand
Smooth and sleek.
As I looked at it
My hand became gnarled
The stone was killing me
My body just lay there
All twisted and dead.

Joseph Kenneth Lunt (12)
Meole Brace School

Sports

S houting and supporting,
P hysical and panting.
O pposition and opponent,
R oar and rules.
T aunting and teams,
S coring and sportsmanship.

Scott Bentley (11)
Meole Brace School

Humpty Dumpty Ballad

One day Humpty Dumpty went for a walk,
Then he stopped on the way and had a talk,
He saw a brilliant, brand new wall,
He found it hard to climb up because it was too tall
But in the end he found his way up that tall wall.

He sat and he sat until it was dark,
He never got off to go to the park,
Only once that was in his heart,
That was also where he did his creative art.

The next dawn he did a large yawn,
What woke him up was a very loud horn,
He rocked heavily back and forth,
After he rocked for the 20th time,
He fell off that hard brick wall.

An old lady passed and saw that,
Humpty had cracked,
She rang the king, his horses and his men,
They put him back together again.

When the next day came,
He was so much in pain,
He was so ashamed to be alive,
He went back on the wall
And hoped he'd die.

Sasha Rocke (13)
Meole Brace School

A Red Rose Is . . .

A red rose is love blossoming
A red rose is beauty
A red rose is rubies shining on an engagement ring
A red rose is a signal to stop
A red rose is . . .

Rianna Matthews (11)
Meole Brace School

My First Day

My hair in the morning was as daft as a brush,
My tummy was frothing like a bubblebath.
Felt like a stranger in my uniform.
My tie was as tight as a bolt on a screw.

Walking to school I was as cold as ice.
For the first 2 hours I had knees shaking like a leaf.
Break time was like being in the middle of town.
I was thirsty, my mouth was as dry as a bone.

Maths was like counting the change in a bank.
Lunchtime was like queuing in a zoo.
The older ones were as cool as a cucumber.

IT was like using someone else's brain.
History was like being my grandad's dad.
At the end of the day I ran out of school as mad as a hatter.
My bag was as heavy as ten bricks.
But I thought it would have been as light as a feather.

The day went as fast as lightning.
I pushed my bike because its tyre was as flat as a pancake.
My homework was as hard as a wall.

Jack Tomkiss (11)
Meole Brace School

My Best Friend

You are friendly, kind and caring,
Sensitive, loyal and understanding,
Humorous, fun, secure and true,
Always there . . . yes, that's you!

Anna Bevan (13)
Meole Brace School

Arsenal Score Again

'Yes! What a save!'
Lehmann just made an excellent save from Forsell's penalty
He throws it over to
Ashley Cole who passes to
Campbell, Campbell takes on Heskey and chips it over
Upson's head to
Viera who controls it perfectly and then sets
Pires on a run,
He cross the ball in and
Henry volleys it with his left foot!
But it hit the woodwork, it comes out to
Reyes who dribbles it past
Melchiot and let flies with his unfavoured right foot!
   Goal!

Ash Keville (11)
Meole Brace School

Writing A Poem

Here I am sitting, thinking
Silently,
Outside I hear screams and laughter,
'Concentrate,' I say to myself,
Noise is so off-putting,
This is so hard,
Trying to write a poem,
What can I write about?
Where's my imagination?
Perhaps I used it all up
In my art homework,
I need to do this for tomorrow,
Time is running out,
Think!
Yes! At last I have an idea . . .

Charlotte Davies (11)
Meole Brace School

Twisted And Mangled Waste Of Space

It was like when
You have been searching
All night long
For that piece of homework.
Oh where is it? Wish I could find it!
Ah! There it is!

In a blue flash, like a camera flash
It was gone and back and gone again and back.
Ah well, it was rubbish.
I wasn't bothered.

But it was still left there
Still and motionless
Twisted and mangled
Like a dying character on centre stage
Dead, worthless, a waste of space.

Tom Swallow (11)
Meole Brace School

Autumn Times

The glowing fireball beats down upon me,
On the hot autumn day.
The farmers are out in their fields,
Collecting the golden hay.

The sweet-scented flowers, colours of pink and violet,
Coating the fields like a duvet on a bed.
As trees are shedding another coat,
A carpet of multicolour lies out ahead.

The time of year that we all love,
Is finally here thanks to the skies above!

Natalie Fisher (13)
Meole Brace School

My Dog Was Murdered

It was like when you have been searching all night.
It was painful, looking here, looking there.
In fact,
I looked everywhere.
Then I saw the blood . . .
It trailed down an alley, a long, long, dark alley . . .

I started to walk down it,
Its eerie atmosphere sent shivers down my spine.
Brraaa!
'What's that?' I asked myself.

I looked up
And saw a bat as black as the alley.
But still I couldn't find my dog.
The alley came to a dead end,
The blood trail stopped
And there was still no sign of 'Tracey' my dog.
My brain was twisted.

Rob Jones (12)
Meole Brace School

Homeless

There's a man people know who lives on the streets,
He wears rags round his head and rags round his feet.
At his side is his dog, limp and lifeless,
Its teeth all yellow, its fur a tangled mess.
He sits there hour after hour, not a penny to his name,
He begs people for money, but the outcome's still the same.
People look at him like dirt,
Like they just scraped him off their shoe,
But he's no different from people like me and you.
No family to love, no family to be loved by,
People hate him so much, he just wishes he'd die.

Eleanor Smith (13)
Meole Brace School

Falling Into Darkness

It was like when you had been searching all night,
My brain gets glued into your head;

I can't think,
Animals are zooming all around me.
How can I continue with all this?
I am stuck.

The theatre was buzzing with excited people.
What is happening in this red blur?
What is happening?

How is it going to stop?
My mind twisted into a big knot.
I need to get out of here,
I am stuck.
No one is like me.
I fall!

Lucy Cockill (11)
Meole Brace School

Why?

When birds go by,
You wonder why,
Why do they get to fly?
We don't; we watch them fly by, in the sky.

Why do slugs go so slow?
We will never know,
Why get eaten by a crow?
Just let them grow and grow.

There was a mouse that lived in a shed,
It had big eyes with a tint of red,
Every day he expected to get fed,
By his owner, Mr Ted.

Luke Edge (13)
Meole Brace School

My First Day

In the morning I woke up
And my tummy was turning
And it was giving me butterflies
I felt like I was going to be sick.

When I put my school uniform on
My tie was strangling me
But it soon loosened up
And I felt a lot better.
After a while I was a bit excited.

At school I was very nervous
I had lots of worries, like if my teachers were going to be horrible
And if I would say their name right.
But in the end it all came together
And I am happy right this minute.

Rebecca Dowley (12)
Meole Brace School

Lyle

L ikes going on holiday to Portugal. Been 3 times.
Y ellow was my favourite colour, but I have gone off it a bit.
L oves football.
E nglish is my strongest subject, as I got a high 5 level in my SATs.

Lyle Sambrook (11)
Meole Brace School

Cherries!

Mm, mm,
Red cherries
Juicy cherries, slurp, slurp
Fruity tastes form inside your mouth
Yummy!

Anouzka Lowrie-Herz (11)
Meole Brace School

What Was It Like?

It was like when you have been
searching all night; it was
dark and cold, you could
see nothing.

It was like you were in a blank
room; nothing there apart
from the stairs. They were
shining ever so brightly
like bees collecting pollen
from the flowers.

The moon looked like it
was dancing among
as if it was in a musical
at the theatre twisted in
to them like balls of wool.

Jessica Gough (13)
Meole Brace School

A Limerick!

There once was a young fellow called Spike,
He rode on an old rusty bike.
He punctured his tyre,
On a piece of barbed wire,
And now he's riding a trike!

Chris Ferris (12)
Meole Brace School

Haiku!

Butterflies do fly
Caterpillars do scuttle
And humans *destroy!*

Vicky Roberts (12)
Meole Brace School

I Feel

It was like when you have been searching all night
As I stand here I feel like a bumblebee looking for some honey
I feel like a bird searching for a worm
I feel like a blue whale looking for big, juicy fish
I feel like a man searching for a loved one who has left his heart
I feel like I am stuck, I am stuck,
I am stuck, I am stuck, I am stuck
A lion in a Roman theatre, everyone is looking at me
I am being attacked, I am stuck
I am stuck, I am stuck, I am stuck
My life is twisted, I don't know what to do or where to look
For I am stuck, I am stuck, I am lost forever
I am stuck, I am stuck
I will never find what I am looking for
Everything is gone.

Luca Furio (12)
Meole Brace School

Food

I love food
Must eat the food
I have it on take-out
I have it homemade
Finished.

John Goodall (13)
Meole Brace School

Sunset

In the sky before night.
A candle as large as the moon,
Casts a shadow of pink.

Lucas Taylor (12)
Meole Brace School

My First Day At School

My stomach churning with butterflies,
Wondering what it will be like,
It will be nothing like my old school,
I'll have to get used to the idea that,
I'll be in the youngest year,
Not the oldest.

I hope I'll get a nice form tutor,
And I'll hopefully make some new friends,
My family tell me this,
But I know they're all as scared as me.
I wonder what I'll do if I get lost?
What if I get a detention on my first day?

Will the work be hard?
What if I get told off?
What will my form tutor be like?
All these questions will be answered soon,
All of my friends will probably be as nervous as me!
I'll be alright once I get there,
I'm sure I will.

Sian Owen (11)
Meole Brace School

Steve The Snail

There once was a snail,
Who delivered the mail,
His name was Postman Steve
Who never delivered on Christmas Eve
But was always a very sad snail.

Polly-Anna Lloyd (12)
Meole Brace School

Heartbreak

I never thought,
That I could love something,
So much, I wish it would just go away.

For what I love has a huge heart,
A heart I cannot look after.

This loving creature is not a human,
But an animal with a stable.

As I stand in front of her,
And stroke her,
Her breath warms my bitterly cold hands.
My throat fills with emotion,
And my eyes start to sting.

My mum calls from the car,
'Hurry up! It's getting late.'

That's when my heart starts to hurt,
As I walk away from her stable,
And she disappears into the darkness.

Grace Meehan (12)
Moreton Hall School

Spider

Thrust against its web
It silently creeps, seeking out its prey,
Its brittle, spindly legs wrapped around the stickiness of strings,
Its breath as silent and cold as a winter's day.
Its body as tough as a suit of armour, just glazed,
The musty smell surrounds the room and sticks to the walls,
Getting caught up in the web,
It watches with beady eyes, as a figure approaches,
Getting closer, closer, closer, *squish!*
Eight legs are scattered.

Katie Christy (12)
Moreton Hall School

Bonfire Night

Our fire is burning
The black smoke withers to the heavens
The dancing flames prance and leap over the burning logs
As the ash floats down
It touches a delicate cheek
My toes tingle with warmth all the way up my body
I hear the crackling and the spit
Floating delicately down to the ground
I can smell the hot dogs being cooked
Making my mouth water with hunger
The sparklers are lit with a great big flash
Going down the lead
As it goes away it seems the fire is floating away
As I am eating my hot dog it is delicious
Slithering down my throat
And as the fire dwindles down
It is time to say it is the end of the night
So we go home
Warm our feet up and snuggle up
And go to sleep and have our dreams.

Katie Stearns (12)
Moreton Hall School

Friends

F orgiveness is the key.
R espect is the way.
I nvolved is her charm.
E verlasting is the love.
N ever break up is the rule.
D ream is the language.
S poken in friendship.

Ebony Ewington (11)
Moreton Hall School

Family

The love,
The comfort,
Which you take for granted.

The roof over your head,
The food on the table,
Which you take for granted.

The shoes on your feet,
The exotic holidays,
Which you take for granted.

The warmth of the house,
The money for clothes,
Which you take for granted.

Think of those who,
Give this to you,
Your family.

Philippa Woodside (12)
Moreton Hall School

My Box
(Based on 'Magic Box' by Kit Wright)

I will put in my box . . .
A hat that blows away in the wind
The treasured moments of walking the gardens
A very important job of changing the calendar
Up on stage as a Christmas pudding
The day Fred Bloggs wrote his name on my English book.

I will put in my box . . .
A poem of yonyons
Spoon bending with a snap
Playing hide-and-seek with a piece of Spam
Mr Ewel's piled-high plate.

Laura Davies (12)
Moreton Hall School

Heaven Weeps

She hovered there,
Helpless, unable to cope,
A weak, young boy
Struggling to live,
At her feet.
When she reached out,
Nothing could be felt,
For she was an angel,
Floating in the chilled air.

Her eyes filled up with tears,
As they trickled down her transparent face,
They dripped onto his delicate skin.
For that moment only,
She looked up,
Up into the heavens above,
Wishing for the little boy's life.

Charlotte Rose Doel (12)
Moreton Hall School

Winter

Fairies float down,
All different,
And land on a diamond lake,
They settle down to rest.

The trees have a new berry,
One that glistens,
The silvery moon,
Floods through the trees.

Down below the diamond shell,
Sometimes stirs,
Of scale and fin,
There's something in the deep.

No sound is heard as the fairies settle,
For sleep.

Jennifer Davies (12)
Moreton Hall School

Dolphin Paradise

Gliding through the exotic waters,
Gracefully flying through the warm air,
Their ever-present smile,
The warmth of their hearts,
We can feel their happiness.

The salted sea water,
Over their soft, smooth, delicate skin,
The sparkle in their big, beautiful eyes.

I can hear them crackling,
Communicating,
What are they saying?

The scent of their fishy breath,
It sends me to paradise.

They travel to find new places,
New food,
New friends,
A new type of happiness.

Lucy Emberton (12)
Moreton Hall School

My Friend

Secret keeper
Sweet sharer
Good listener
Friendship giver
Sport lover
Flower picker
Birthday bumper
Shoe shopper
Daydreamer
Sweet carer
Baby hugger.

Chloe England (11)
Moreton Hall School

The Voyage Of The Family Album

Smell the rushes all around,
Snaps! A smile never found.

Swimming in a wood of trees,
Bang! A holiday in the Pyrenees.

Stop, a rest as we twirl the page,
Wham! A lunch with Auntie Pam.

Running fingers up and down
Snap! The family album's found.

Open the book, open your eyes,
Snap, bang, twirl, surprise!

Jemma Moore (12)
Moreton Hall School

All In All My Best Friend

Activity lover
Support worker
Tennis basher
Flower picker
Cuddle giver
Birthday bumper
Daring jumper
Bouncy giggler
Funny fiddler
Bubble blower
And all in all
My best friend.

Isabelle Whiteley (11)
Moreton Hall School

Friends

F riends are always there for you and having fun,
R oaring loudly in the playground,
I nvolves you with everything that she does,
E nds up having an argument,
N aughty, devil-like and cheeky,
D readful and not listening and then tells your secrets. What
S ort of a friend is she?

Chantelle Fry (11)
Moreton Hall School

Friendship

F orever following fast, in your footsteps,
R evving to get going,
I njecting energy into your day,
E nthusiastically cheering you on,
N ever abandons you when you need her most,
D efinitely a good friend!

Jodie Nicholson (11)
Moreton Hall School

My Best ?

Careful listener,
Secret sharer,
Always together,
Steady player,
Funky dresser,
Good carer,
Quick helper,
Cheerful singer,
Friends forever!

Barba Hedley (12)
Moreton Hall School

My Best Friend

F orgives you for something bad you have done
R esponsible when you give her something
I nvolves you in everything that is going on
E ntertains you and makes you laugh when you are down
N ice to you and friendly
D efends you when someone is being horrible to you
S uch a great friend.

Annabel Kempsey (11)
Moreton Hall School

Friends Forever

F riends forever
R eady to cheer you up when you need it
I ndividual time together all the time
E ndless fun together
N o arguments just friendship
D oing what they can to help
S ometimes you need them for a shoulder to cry on.

Tabatha Leanne Clark (11)
Moreton Hall School

Friend

F riends forever.
R espects me and my ways.
I s loving and caring.
E nters me into their heart.
N ever mean.
D eep friendship all the time.

Olivia Towers (11)
Moreton Hall School

Chocolate

Mmm . . . chocolate, chocolate
Yummy chocolate I want
You know you're torturing me.

Chocolate, chocolate
I want you now
I can't get you off my mind
The sound of you crunching, crackling in my watering mouth.

Chocolate, chocolate
Stop it now
The smell of you is scrumdiddlyumptious.

Chocolate, chocolate
I've got you now
In my mouth you go
You're like a party in my mouth
With the chocolatey smell, mmm . . .
Into my tummy you go.

Georgina Mannering (12)
Phoenix School

Chocolate Poem

As the chocolate went in my mouth,
You could hear me munch.
Listen to that lovely sound, crunch, crunch,
When I opened another,
The soft and creamy taste,
When I finished it, it went over my face,
Mmm . . . don't you just love chocolate?

Yasmin Sangha (12)
Phoenix School

Mum's Chocolate

Chocolate is great
Chocolate is nice
The temptation is there but I can't eat it
I can't eat it, it's not mine
But it is speaking to me saying,
'Eat me, eat me.'

I like chocolate, the way it melts in your mouth
I like the way chocolate smells
I like the way chocolate sounds when you open it
But most of all
I like the way it tastes.

I still can't eat it
It's just sitting there on the table
But it's not mine
Temptation's got the better of me
As I open it my mum walks through the door,
'Get your hands off my chocolate!'

Hannah Fowles (13)
Phoenix School

Chocolate Poem

As my mum brought it out,
I could smell it with my snout,
When the saliva came into my throat,
I dribbled all down my coat,
I watched it looking at me,
It said, 'I'm gorgeous, can't you see?'
After I'd stripped it and took a bite,
I was in Heaven like a runaway kite,
It was a Galaxy delight.

Jack Evans (12)
Phoenix School

Food

Champion cheese is what I love the most
Sprinkled on my beans on toast
Cheese is the best for sure
All over my Croque Monsieur
Melting, bubbling on the bread
Better than a day in bed
Cheese, the mighty cheese, the great
I've never found a better mate.

Boisterous burgers bounce on the grill
Then onto my plate, oh what a thrill!
Covered in sauce, in a bap
Down my front and on my lap
But I don't waste it, that's for sure
Pile them on and gimme some more!

Happy hot dogs on my plate
Better eat them before it's too late
Sitting there smiling, so proud
Cover them in sauce and eat them all down
Who cares about calories, about weight?
We can't live without food so grab another plate!

Lauren Cox (12)
Phoenix School

Chocolate Is . . .

Chocolate is golden and creamy
It's milky and scrumdiddlyumptious
It's like a party in my mouth
Mmm, I love chocolate
Into my mouth you go, mmm.

Stefan Ecclestone (12)
Phoenix School

Chocolate

Yummy, scrummy chocolate bunny
Let it melt in my mouth
Chewy, gooey, even screwy
It's gone down nice
In my belly, feet and wellies.

Lovely, nice, made with ice
Mars, Bounty, Smarties too
Whichever you eat you need to chew
Small and round, big and thick
Can't I just have a little bit?

Lollies and rock,
Come from my pock
In my mouth, down it goes
Watch out belly, watch out toes
Now my poem comes to an end
Share your chocolate with a friend.

Daniel Benting (12)
Phoenix School

Chocolate, Chocolate

Chocolate, chocolate
Everybody likes chocolate
It taunts you, it laughs at you
But then you get to eat it
Chocolate, chocolate
Everybody likes chocolate
It looks dairy and tastes milky
And it's very chewy
Chocolate, chocolate
I really do like chocolate.

Nathan Musgrave (13)
Phoenix School

Chocolate

It's evil
I need it
It feels so smooth
It sounds crinkly, crackly, crunchy
It smells so special and milky
It looks delicious
It tastes like I'm in Heaven.

One more
Two more
Three more
No more
I've gone from Heaven to Hell
I miss the brown chocolate fun
I'll have to open another box.

Chris Johnson (12)
Phoenix School

Food

Food is nice,
Especially chicken curry with rice,
This will make you pleased,
But mostly better than smelly old cheese.

Sunday dinner, the one of them all,
You could eat it anywhere, even in the hall,
Fish and chips,
The salt tingles on your lips.

Chocolate and sweets,
Are always nice for a treat,
Food is cool and food is fun,
But always eat it in the lovely sun!

April Morris (13)
Phoenix School

Food

Food is tasty,
Food is good,
Food, food, food,
Food for people,
Food for animals,
Food, food, food,
Food is different shapes,
Food is different sizes,
Food, food, food,
Food has different tastes,
Food has different smells,
Food, food, food,
Food tastes good,
Food tastes bad,
Food, food, food,
Food is shaped normal,
Food is shaped mad,
Food, food, food,
Food comes in bags,
Food comes in boxes,
Food, food, food,
Food for me,
Food for you,
Food, food, food.

Lewis Hocking (11)
Phoenix School

My Favourite Foods

Licking liquorice, long and luscious.
Passionate, pounding pizza.
Hideous, hot, hairy hot dogs.
Clever, cool, colourful cake.
Chunky, charming, cheeky chocolate.

Shannon Tranter (11)
Phoenix School

A Little Box Of Treasure!

A little box of treasure is a wonderful delight.
Each individual chocolate, creamy and light.
The temptation is irresistible as I can see it tastes yummy.
Wouldn't those lumps of Heaven be lovely in my tummy?

They tease me by shouting, 'You know you want to!'
Oh, what am I going to do?
They make irritating sounds then;
As I untwist the foil wrapper my heart suddenly bounds.

Rustle, crackle, crinkle, crunch!
The sound of autumn leaves slowly reveals.
The dreamy sensations break free from their seals.

Mmmmm! They smell so divine,
Their smell is gorgeous and luscious,
That one is definitely mine!

Then into the mouth open wide,
I really cannot describe how wonderful they taste as they slide.
Melting softly, sweet as I lick,
The flavoursome and perfect chocolate is extremely thick.

One . . two . . . three . . . whoops! It's gone.
But never mind, there's still more for me.
So reaching like there's no tomorrow,
I grab them all to save their sorrow!

Jessica Hayward (13)
Phoenix School

Stor 6

Runny, yolky eggs, sliding down your throat,
Orange, juicy, jumping beans, jump from side to side.
Sizzling, chunky chips, spitting in your face.
6 silly sausages, sizzling in the pan.
Tasty, flappy flapjacks, melting on your tongue.

Danielle Antonsen (11)
Phoenix School

Food, Food, Delicious Food

Food, food, delicious food,
You eat it when you want to, depending on your mood.
Peas, sausages, bacon, chips,
Eat it all, then lick your lips.

Food, food, delicious food,
You eat it when you want to, depending on your mood.
Chips, tomatoes, apples and bread,
Eat it all, then go to bed.

Food, food, delicious food,
You eat it when you want to, depending on your mood.
Chocolate cake and banana splits,
Eat it all, you won't get fit.

Food, food, delicious food,
You eat it when you want to, depending on your mood.
Mashed potatoes, carrots, broccoli, gravy,
Eat it all in the navy.

Food, food, delicious food,
You eat it when you want to, depending on your mood.
Tinned stuff, soft stuff, fresh stuff, hard stuff,
I've eaten it all now, that's just tough!

Emily Buttery (12)
Phoenix School

Food

The colour of curry clashes in your mouth
The beef begs with beauty
Harmless ham hops away in my mouth
Posh potatoes poke each other
Ice-cold ice cream is too cold for me.

Nathan Wilkinson (11)
Phoenix School

It's Food!

Sausage
Chips
Bacon
Beans
Egg
Custard
Runner beans
Spaghetti
Pasta
Chips and
Bread
Salt and
Pepper
And a duck's head
Cottage pie
Broccoli
Sprouts
Carrots
That's all for tea!
Now for lunch
I'd start with punch
Ham
Cheese
Frozen peas
Toasted bread
Margarine
Pizza
'Tatoes
Crisps and
Wedges
Followed by
Next-door's hedges
Stir fry
Chicken
Turkey
Peppers
Onions
And a sweet birdie

Now I'm full up, down to my knee,
Nothing else can go in me!

Ben Folger (12)
Phoenix School

My Favourite Foods

Cake is casual, characteristic and full of charm
Sweet corn is shy, shameless, sly, satisfactory and slender
Pizza is particularly passionate and perfect
Hot dogs are handsome, harmless and heavenly hot
Burgers are blissfully beefy, beloved and beautiful.

Stephanie Jean Rippon (11)
Phoenix School

Food

Brussels sprouts are horrible,
Along with carrots,
I hate chocolate,
I hate cabbage.

I like ice cream,
It is the best,
Along with crisps,
These are the best.

I like spaghetti,
It wriggles all over the place.
I like it with tomato sauce,
These are the best.

I like peas with minced meat,
I would like to have a feast,
With melted ice cream and
A jam tart underneath.

I like food,
It keeps me alive.
I like McDonald's, it is the best,
These foods are the best.

Natasha Griffin (12)
Phoenix School

Food!

Creamy, chocolatey, custardy-covered cakes,
Green grapes, gurgling geese,
Cockerel, cluck, crow, crazy claws,
Carrots are cool, crunchy, crazy, cranky creatures,
Carrots, cress, cucumber, mixed to make a cranky crumble.

Gemma Machin (11)
Phoenix School

Strawberries

Sour strawberries,
Super, sour strawberries,
Super, sour, Shrewsbury strawberries,
Super, sour, Shrewsbury, sugary strawberries,
Super, sour, Shrewsbury, sugary, soft strawberries,
Super, sour, Shrewsbury, sugary, soft, soggy strawberries,
Soft, soggy, Shrewsbury, sugary strawberries
Are really super sour.

Laura Oliver-Day (12)
Phoenix School

Food!

Shoving the food in my mouth
Just piling up every spoonful I eat
Can never stop eating
It's too good to leave
For some reason I can't get a breath
I think there's too much in my mouth
I need to put it somewhere
I started to choke
Then it all spurted out
All over my dad's plate.

Rosie May (13)
Phoenix School

Food

Chips, chips, crunchy chips,
Beans, beans, bouncing beans,
Pizza, pizza, lovely pizza,
Chocolate, chocolate, I eat chocolate,
Crisps, brittly, crackly crisps.

Kyle Perry (11)
Phoenix School

Sunday Lunch

We sit down at the long, oak table
We hear the chairs squeaking
As people sit down
Mum comes through with a plate
Piled with tender chicken
Bob comes through with a bowlful of potatoes
Tripping over the cat's tail
The potatoes go everywhere!
One rolled out the front door
Dad said, 'Are we eating out today?'

Robert Leigh (13)
Phoenix School

Food!

Crispy, chewy, crunchy too
That's my dish designed for you
Nice and hot in a curry pot.

Crispy, chewy, crunchy
Chicken
Chomping in my cheeks
It just tastes like old men's *feet!*
Crispy, chewy, crunchy!

Aimee Glover (13)
Phoenix School

Sausage!

S ickly, sizzling sausages frying in the pan!
A nxious to gobble
U nusual to leave a scrap
S oapy, saucy sausages nearly all gone
A ppetites for everyone
G obbling them quickly down
E veryone wants more, more, more!

Samantha Mathars (12)
Phoenix School

Pizza And Chips

Dinner, dinner, come down all
it's pizza and chips with
lovely red sauce. Runny
and red, thick and said
to be the best ever
sauce there is.

Salt and vinegar
pepper too
all mixed
together
which makes
a witch's
brew.

After there's
pudding
yummy and
scrummy. It's
ice cream
and sauce.

Blobby and slobby
there's not enough
for my tummy
and it's disappearing
fast.
All that was
there is now
in the master's lair which
is the digester from Hell.

Andrew Thorpe (12)
Phoenix School

Food, Food, Yummy Food

When our tummy mumbles
It's crying out with hunger
We've got to eat some food
Before it sounds like thunder.

What shall we have to eat?
Chocolate, crisps or cake?
Let us have all three
It really does sound great.

But what about when Mum comes home?
We'll be having meat and sprouts
Roasters, peas and Yorkshire puds
And a pudding without doubt.

I'll just have to have a snack now
Perhaps a piece of cake
Or should I have the chocolate?
It's a choice I'll have to make

To stop my tummy rumbling
And not to upset Mum
I'll have to have my tea soon
And it better all be gone.

I'll have the chocolate later
Sneak it off to bed
And sit up in my room alone
With my covers over my head!

Amy Huntington (13)
Phoenix School

Chocolate Heaven

I looked at the wrapper
Slowly I heard it say, 'Eat me.'
Miss Wallman said we couldn't eat it yet!
I was so hungry
I imagined it in my mouth
Melting slowly
A party on my tongue
The creamy texture
The caramel is bursting out of the chocolate
She said we could open it but we couldn't eat it!
I was tempted to take a chunk out of the chocolate
The time would come to eat
I could smell the heavenly milky chocolate
My five favourite words
Now you can eat it! Mmm, yummy.

William Davies (13)
Phoenix School

Strawberries

S weet and sour
T ummy treats
R andomly rammed in my mouth
A bsolutely sweet
W ild but wicked
B etter than burgers
E ager
R osy-red
R umbling in my tummy
I deal every day
E mergency to buy some
S ugar on top is the *best!*

Kirsty Edwards (12)
Phoenix School

Yummy

Chocolate is so scrummy
It's just where it should be -
In my tummy
Yummy, yummy, yummy

Red, yellow, gold and blue
Makes me want to chew
Toffee, caramel, goo!
Just like I'm going to

Rustle, rustle, rustle
Makes me want to tug and tustle
Chocolate is my desire
I'm honest, not a liar

Galalastic it's so fantastic
Eat, eat, eat
It's one tasty treat
For me and you to eat.

Ryan Cooke (11)
Phoenix School

Chocolate

I love chocolate, me, yeah
Mars, Crunchie, Cadbury's too
Anything will do
It all looks so dreamy
When I put it into my mouth
The chocolate smell is there
I feel it melting on my tongue
In a few seconds it's gone
The teacher's coming, what will I do?
It's too late
I'm doomed.

Luke Antonsen (12)
Phoenix School

Chocolate Poem

I want! Give it!
It tastes so creamy and juicy
It looks so sexy and bumpy
It's so melty and Marsalicious
It's saying, 'Eat me all over.'
It is so soft and it tastes divine
It is Heaven
It sounds so lovely
It is the last one so *give it!*

Lewis Hayward (11)
Phoenix School

Chocolate Delight

Chocolate has different tastes
Smooth, buttery and sugary stuff
But I don't care what they are
I can't get enough!
I sit on the sofa eating more
Mint ones, toffee ones, fudge too
Caramels, coconut, too many to choose
Crunchy truffles, Turkish delights
They're all so good, I could munch all night.

Haydn Coates (11)
Phoenix School

Tucker!

'Hey, what's for tucker?' the Aussies say
'I want grubs, by the way,
If I can't I want a barbie,
With some sliced salami,
Maybe a sausage or a sarnie,
I think I'm just plain barmy!'

Georgia Gadd (12)
Phoenix School

Chocolate

Yummy, sitting on my desk was a lovely piece of chocolate,
I want to eat it but I wasn't allowed,
My mouth was watering,
I was very impatient but I couldn't,
Miss was teasing us by not letting us have one until the end,
Finally we eat it,
It was fabdicious,
I want another!

Thomas Byrne (11)
Phoenix School

La Chocolàt

Creamy, tempting, milk delight,
Rippling, rich chocolàt,
Bubbling, melting, wrong but right,
A cascading wall of chocolàt.

A dreamy, rich sensation,
Teasing, taunting chocolàt,
A melting, tempting, fab creation,
A heavenly treasure, chocolàt.

Rachel Smith (13)
Phoenix School

Chocolate Munch

Sitting there on the shelf,
Just ready to grab and munch.
Just peel the wrapper and take a bite,
And listen for the *crunch*.
But luckily that's not me,
'Cause I've got something better.
A king-size Crunchie, ready to munch,
Stuffed up the sleeve of my sweater.

Ashley Kitson (12)
Phoenix School

Chocolate

The taunting temptation,
To watch it lie and laugh at you.
To want to rip open the foil to reveal a buried treasure.
The dread about calories and diets,
And the little voice screaming, 'Just one won't hurt!'
But you know it will,
The smell's getting to you.
The rich, haunting smell, floating gently on the breeze.
It's laughing harder now,
Knowing you're scared to eat it.
Until you finally grab it,
Pull apart the foil,
And throw it quickly in your mouth.
Then you're angry,
Because it was the last one in the box.

Laura Greenfield (13)
Phoenix School

Chocolate Poem

Chocolate.
Just sitting there,
Perfectly shaped, perfectly formed.
Thinking.
Should I? Why shouldn't I?
Just one bite won't hurt.
Would it?
The dreamy smell taking over.
The silky-smooth taste flooding in me.
The warmth tickling my insides.
So moreish.
So mmmmmm.
So gone.

Laura Onions (13)
Phoenix School

Chocolate

Tempting and tasty, it sits on the desk,
Waiting for my mouth to smother its chocolatey surface.
It's screaming, 'Eat me, eat me!'
Yummy, yummy, yummy,
I can't wait,
My fingers grab it,
And . . .
Gulp, it's gone.
What's happened to the chocolate?
Where's it gone? What's happened?
I'll hide the wrapper before anybody sees,
She'll go mad,
Bonkers!

Danielle Horton (11)
Phoenix School

Chocolate

Teasing and tempting, it sat on the desk
I sat, impatient, waiting for the time to come
My mouth started watering with temptation
It sat there haunting me all the time
The brown, shiny wrapper made things worse
It made me all warm and comfortable inside
Its sexy eyes staring at me
I'm being tormented by the lovely chocolate
The chocolate is shouting, 'Eat me!'
I'm trying not to eat it but it's so tempting
Then the special moment comes
Miss says, 'You can *eat it!'*
And when the chocolate touched my lips
It felt great!

Sam Holding (11)
Phoenix School

Delicious, Lovely Food

Food is delicious,
Food is tasty,
Food is the best,
Put your teeth in a pastry!

You need food to live,
There's a whole variety to choose from,
Start off by putting your flour in a sieve,
And now get baking!

Baking food is fun,
Especially when you're baking a bun,
But the best part of it all,
Is when you wait to taste it, it makes you drool!

I love food,
So please don't be rude,
Don't smell your feet,
I'm trying to eat!

Alexander Edwards (12)
Phoenix School

Chocolate

I like chocolate very much,
It's brown and dark and yummy,
It's never in my mouth too long,
It slides down to my tummy!

It looks and smells,
And tastes so great,
It makes my life complete,
It is the 'bestest' food of all,
For anyone to eat!

Tom Seymour (13)
Phoenix School

A Day In The Life Of A Pizza

In the grocery store he waits
A pizza with no love or hate
Covered in cheese and tomato sauce
No toppings, this pizza is good enough for a horse.

Every day they go
But now it's this pizza's time to say adios
Taken away from the freezer
He thought it would be easier
Boy, was he mistaken.

He was unwrapped in an unusual way
And put into the cave of extreme heat
And when it was done
He opened his eye
And found he had already been digested.

Alexander Edwards (12)
Phoenix School

Gooey, Sticky Chocolate!

Out of all the food that I adore,
Chocolate is the least.
The health affects I really abhor
And the junk food spots are beasts.

Sticking in the back of your mouth like glue,
Oozing in the cracks between your teeth,
While others slobber, drool and chew,
Chocolate just brings me grief.

So although you all say it's the best,
It just poisons your blood,
So please , give me a rest,
I hate it, it's just no good.

Lyndsey Pitchford
Phoenix School

Food Is Fantastic!

F ood is great, food is fab with
O melette and
O range cheesecake, now that's fab
D inner is fish and chips, now that's yummy, always filling
my tummy.

I ce cream for pud
S trawberry flavoured is good.

F ood is the world, food is your life
A nything to your delight
N othing is bad, don't listen to your dad
T ake my advice, I'm right
A pple crumble is so yummy
S pecial sauce makes it very nice and scrummy
T ime for dessert, now what shall I have?
I 'll have the best thing ever made
C hocolate biscuits, now they're the ones to grab. They're
absolutely fab!

Nicole Dickenson (12)
Phoenix School

Food

Food means a lot to me,
Chips and beans are great for my tea.
Chocolate, McDonald's, Burger King too,
Don't worry, I'll leave some for you.

Plums, apples and strawberries with cream,
Cherry pie is such a dream.
Carrots and meat in a lovely stew,
Don't worry I'll leave some for you.

Pizza, chicken, fish and chips,
Chicken nuggets in a tomato dip.
All this food is yummy too,
Don't worry, I won't leave some for you!

Sophie Needle (12)
Phoenix School

National Poem Day

Yummy, yummy, yum,
Food for my tum,
A boogie, boogie, bum,
Lots of food and rum.

Beany, beany, beans,
Eggy, eggy, bread,
Salty, salty, chips,
That's all that can be said.

Pasty, pasty, pasta,
Cabbagey, cabbagey, cabbage,
Veggie, veggie, carrots,
Sprouts are very savage.

Jacky, jacky, potato,
Chicky, chicky, chicken,
Spicy, spicy, onion,
That's all for my kitchen.

Alex Hallewell (12)
Phoenix School

A Poem About Food!

When a bag of gorgeous chips,
Touch your lovely, luscious lips,
Oh, they taste so, so great,
When they're for tea, you won't be late.

I know a girl named Betty
And she really hates spaghetti.
But I think that it tastes nice,
Especially with my spicy rice.

Pizza has some lovely toppings,
Cheese and tomatoes are always popping,
Out of the pizzas I see,
But never in my life have I seen peas,
On any pizza I have seen.

Erika Peake (12)
Phoenix School

How Great Is Food!

Food is that thing
You eat off your plate
Snack when you're down
Eat if you're out

Food can be found in many kinds
Sweet like chocolate
Savoury like crisps
Normal like carrots
Or weird like banana soup

Food is great
It keeps us alive
It's there when we want
It stops all our hunger
So I have reached the conclusion
That food is *great!*

Harriet Blower (12)
Phoenix School

Tomatoes

Tomatoes, tomatoes everywhere,
Upstairs, downstairs,
Everywhere.
Circle ones,
Red ones,
Crunchy ones too,
Juicy ones,
Sweet ones,
Everywhere.
I don't know which ones we're going to share.

Jodie Hewitt (12)
Phoenix School

Chocolate

So good, yet so bad
It's enough to drive you mad
Temptation overruling
Can't stop myself from drooling
It's so wrong, yet so right
Oh, just a little bite
Crunchy, smooth and creamy
Sticky, rich and dreamy
Mmmm honey, a mini pot of gold
Stuff my tea, let it go cold
'K K K calories'
Into the chopper and down the slide
Keeps my taste buds satisfied.
Mmmm chocolate.

Kristy Williams (13)
Phoenix School

Food Poem

I love food

L ovely pasta, cheese, beans and peas,
O h, what a wonderful feast for me,
V eggie is alright, pudding is the best,
E very single scrap I eat, to show I love it all

F or every single pea I eat, my dad gives me more,
O h lovely food, oh lovely food, I will eat it all my life,
O h lovely food, I love it so much,
D elicious food is good to eat, what a treat.

I love food.

Rebekah Hughes (12)
Phoenix School

Food Poem

For starters:
Garlic bread that's cooked, an unappetising shade of black
And watery soup from a cook who has lost his knack.
Then some fizzy drink that tastes like they've got the wrong sort
                                                                of Coke,
'The main course had better be better,' I croak.

For the main course:
Some chicken that was a dark shade of brown
And some Yorkshire pudding that really got me down.
The rest of the dish, I think had been burgled,
'The dessert had better be better,' I gurgled.

For dessert:
A sickly brown lump sitting on a plate,
My appetite it failed to sate.
On top of this were some Smarties
That had obviously passed their sell-by date.

'£43.50,' cried the waiter,
'OK, but I'm not coming back later.'
And so I drove home, choking on mints,
I've never gone back there since.

Jamie Wynn (12)
Phoenix School

Chocolate

Lots and lots of chocolate
It's all around my face
I must look a disgrace
Go on, take another
It is so scrumptious
Scrumdiddlyumptious
Fill the wrappers with stones
They'll never know!

Jessica Jarvis (12)
Phoenix School

Chocolate

It's whispering to me, saying,
'Eat me, eat me, eat me.'
I hear crackling and crinkling,
Also rustling of the foil.
It's telling me, 'Go on,
You know you want to.'
I'm now hearing my tummy rumbling.

It's got a lovely texture,
Creases upon creases, creases upon creases.
I can feel my heart beating,
Waiting for the chocolate to slip down my throat.
I feel happy as can be
And I feel that it's looking at me.

I'm thinking to myself, *mmm, mmm,*
It's purposely tempting me.
I'm just too tempted,
It makes me think I'm in Heaven.

Gavin Brooks (12)
Phoenix School

Food Is The Best!

Food can be shaped like a clown,
That looks down.
Food can be flat like bread,
That goes in through the front of your head.
Food can be big like roast turkey,
Or it could be an American beef jerky.
Food can be nice like cake,
Or horrible like fish from the bottom of the lake.
But whichever way,
Let's just say, 'Hey, hey, hey,'
Because food is here to stay.

Josh Weale (11)
Phoenix School

Food!

A is for apple
B is for banana
C is for chocolate
D is for Doritos
E is for egg
F is for fish
G is for gammon
H is for ham
I is for ice cream
J is for jelly
K is for kiwi
L is for lemon sherbets
M is for mango
N is for nuts
O is for orange
P is for pizza
Q is for quail eggs
R is for roast chicken
S is for sandwiches
T is for turkey
U is for ucky!
V is for vegetables
W is for wheat
X is for e-xotic food
Y is for yoghurt
Z is for zest!

Jodie Hayward (12)
Phoenix School

An A-Z Of Food!

Food!
There's:
  A pples, hard and crunchy.
  B ananas, soft and mushy, ew!
  C risps, all different flavours, yum!
  D oughnuts, sweet and sugary.
  E ggs, fried or scrambled, yum!
  F ish, salmon, cod, ew!
  G rapes, small and squishy.
  H am, smoked and wafer-thin, yum!
  I ce cream, cold and melted, ew not!
  J am, sticky, strawberry.
  K iwi fruit, seedy and slimy, ew!
  L emons, sharp and sour, nice!
  M elons, wet and juicy.
  N uts, hard and horrible, ew!
  O range, sweet and juicy, yum!
  P ineapple, prickly and zesty.
  Q uails' eggs, blue and weird, ew!
  R aisins, small and dry, yum!
  S ugar, sweet and sticky.
  T ea, totally boring, ew!
  U gli fruit, weird and foreign, ew!
  V ermicelli, tiny and tasty.
  W afers, light and crispy, ew!
  X - ?
  Y oghurt, creamy and flavoured, yum!
  Z - don't ask me, OK?

Natalie James (11)
Phoenix School

Food, Glorious Food!

Food, food, it's the best thing ever
I won't stop eating, no not ever
Chocolate bars and crispy cakes
Are lots more fun for me to bake.

Carrots, sprouts are not so yummy
I would rather have something else to fill my tummy
Like toffee apples or chewy sweets
Which I like to have as a treat.

Food, food, it's the best thing ever
I won't stop eating, no not ever
Fish and chips or Maccie D's
Are ten times nicer than mushy peas.

Food, food, it's the best thing ever
I won't stop eating, no not ever.

Jodie Thomas (12)
Phoenix School

Friendship

Friendship is like a golden chain,
That links our friends so dear
And like a rare and precious jewel,
It's treasured more each year.
It's clasped together firmly,
With a love that's deep and true,
It's rich with happy memories
And fond recollections too.
Time can't destroy the friendship we have,
As years go by and by,
The friendship we share together,
Will last until the day we die.

Sophie Price (11)
Phoenix School

Ahmed!

Ahmed, stop watching telly, you will grow fat!
Having too much chocolate rots teeth, so pack it in.
Meddling with other people's business, stay out, naughty boy!
Ending the day with a lot of racket.
Dribbling over food you never get, *shut up!*

Never making life better, you spoil it.
Using your legs and feet to think you're hard.
Staying up all night playing on the PS2.
Shouting at teachers, won't listen!
Ahmed Hussain always listens to R 'n' B in his house when he
                                                        is bored.
Never punish teachers or blame them when you choose the
                                                        wrong path.

Ahmed Hussain (13)
Phoenix School

My Best Friend And My Ex-Best Friend (Food)

Food is the tastiest thing you have ever had,
Food gives you energy to be a pro-athlete,
Food is the key to cloud nine,
Food takes you straight up to Heaven,
Food leaves a tingly feeling in your mouth,
Food is a never-ending taste,
Food makes you throw up over your homework,
Food is as nasty as your parents,
Food is undoubtedly foul,
Food belongs in the garbage ready to be thrown out,
Food is that English essay you keep putting off,
Food is a goblin lurking under your bed!

Laura Edwards (11)
Phoenix School

Go On, Take A Bite

It lay there on the shelf.
I was thinking to myself,
Shall I just take a bite?
Or will I end up in a fight?
The wrapper was all crispy
And the smell was divine.
But it's not mine!
But now was my chance.
I took another glance.
I could smell the glory.
I reached and grabbed it in my hand
And it didn't look at all bland.
I slipped the wrapper off
And yum!
I think he'll have to buy another one!

Rachel Maddocks (12)
Phoenix School

Chocolate

Chocolate is yummy
For your tummy,
When I eat a Malteser,
It's a real tongue-pleaser,
When I eat a Crunchie,
It makes me munchy,
When I eat a Bounty,
I'm in a different country,
When I eat a Snickers,
The choccie nuts are delicious,
When I eat a Dairy Milk,
Its taste is pure velvet silk.

William Bradley (12)
Phoenix School

Chocolate Disaster

I peel off the wrapper and smell . . .
Mmmm
It smells creamy
It smells chocolatey
But I cannot have it!
Not until I've had my tea.

My mum puts it back in the wrapper
And seals it shut in the fridge.
It's worse than torture.
It's worse than being strangled!
All I can think about is chocolate.
I eat my tea as quick as I can.

Yes!
I can finally have it.
But noooo!
I drop it and the . . .
Dog gets it first!

Reiss Sudden (12)
Phoenix School

A Poem About Food

My favourite food is brunch:
Eggs, chips, beans, sausages,
Is it time for lunch?
Rats, bats, maggots, snails, yum-yum,
Munch, munch, they all go in my tum,
Hair of a bear, snails and puppy-dog tails in my belly,
Ben, Lewis and Tom, chopped up and mixed with jelly.
Put all these in a mixing bowl, now add a witch's mole,
Apples, bananas, oranges, grapes - all horrible.
Now I'm off to my mates.
Do you want a bite?
It has rats, bats and moles all in a bowl,
Have a bite, you know it's right.

Christopher Weavill (12)
Phoenix School

A Perfection Known As Chocolate

Chocolate, a most alluring food,
To be consumed when you're in the mood,
To have a most delightful treat,
A food you can't elude to eat.

The smell can be heard if you listen closely,
A smell only defined as chocolatey,
Graceful in look and graceful in taste,
A treat too exquisite to waste.

So silky, so smooth, so special to savour,
Unmatched with distinct and delicious flavour,
Liberate it from its captive wrapping,
You know you want to.

A sin maybe, enticing,
The concept of it, mouth-watering,
You want it to last forever,
Unsurpassed.

The cuboid of perfection,
The unexceedable confection,
The delicacy of every nation,
The unrivalled chocolate.

Scott Peters (13)
Phoenix School

Untitled

In your mouth, all so creamy,
Chanting, 'Eat me, eat me.'
As it runs in your mouth it's like Heaven.
Galaxy, Bounty or even Maltesers,
They are all delicious.
My favourite chocolate is an Aero,
Full of bubbles and mint, in your mouth melting,
Sweet and creamy on your tongue.
The next time I have chocolate won't be so long.

Liam Wilkinson (11)
Phoenix School

Food Poem

What food means to me:
I like to eat chicken meat,
Sprouts are the best of the rest,
I like to eat chocolate sweets.

What food means to me:
I like to eat sprouts with meat,
Potatoes are planted,
Chips are made to have with meat.

What food means to me:
I like peas with minced meat,
I like to have a piece,
These are the best.

What food means to me:
Cut up bread,
With a boiled egg,
Is the best!

Kieren Griffin (12)
Phoenix School

Chocolate Poem

Walking to the shop
Thinking what to buy
In the shop, lots to choose
Can't make up my mind.

Scanning along the shelves
At last I've found the one
Handing over pocket money
Finally it's mine.

Chocolate melting in my mouth
Tasting nice and yummy
Soon it's all gone, that went fast
Left with an empty wrapper.

Josh Robinson (11)
Phoenix School

Chocolate

Tempting and teasing, on the desk,
Red and gold wrapper covering it up,
It's like an egg,
An alien's head,
It wants me to eat it,
It stares me in the face,
Jumping at my mouth.

Smooth like skin,
It smells delicious,
It makes my mouth water,
I wish I could eat it, but teacher says no.
I wait and wait until we eat it,
Looking me in the mouth,
On the inside it's nice and creamy.

Finally we can eat it,
It tastes scrumdiddlyumptious,
It melts in my mouth,
It tastes beautiful.

Ryan Trowers (11)
Phoenix School

Temptation

When I see a chocolate, I hear it saying, 'Bite me.'
It looks so tempting and I stare at it, then try to flee.
It is too difficult to ignore its sweet, delicious taste.
I think, *if I don't eat it quick, it would be such a waste.*
I look again. The wrapper's gone, the chocolate's broken free.
I can't resist . . . it's in my mouth and melting - heavenly!

Michael McCallin (13)
Phoenix School

Chocolate - The Nation's Favourite

Some people like to relax sometimes,
Some people go on holidays,
Some people go for a walk,
Some people like to have a good night's sleep,
But I like to relax with a box of chocolates.
Get comfortable, put on your favourite film,
Open the box carefully, so as not to ruin the moment.
The tense seconds as you lift the lid that last few inches.
You can hear them speaking to you,
All the different flavours - coffee, toffee, banoffee and dark,
All saying, *'Eat me,'* and, *'You know you want to.'*
You can smell them - heavenly, dreamy, creamy and divine.
Take one out of the box,
Put it on your tongue.
Don't chew! Just let it melt on your tongue.
Taste the chocolatey, fluffy, sweet, moreish taste.
You're in Heaven,
But then you come back down to Earth,
Until they tempt you again.
Chocolate is and always will be the nation's favourite.

Tom Boneham (13)
Phoenix School

Sweets And Sugar

Sweets, sugar, sweet, sweet custard
I don't want any of that yellow earwax looking like mustard
I like Mars bars, Milky Ways
I'm not having those greens or vitamins, no day, no way
Sugar, sugar, sugar, give it to me
Let me lick those luscious, lip-smacking, lime-flavoured, lovely-looking
                                                        lollies glaring at me
It's chocolate cake calling me to eat it - call me again, repeat it
Feeling kind of podgy, feeling full up, like a bloated, revolting,
                                                        real fat truck.

Lewis Bates (12)
Phoenix School

Chocolate

Watching it hungrily,
It beckons me forward,
Just sitting there in the sun,
Its golden wrapper glistens.
What if it melts?
What would I do?
Its heavenly scent runs through the air,
My mouth begins to water,
My hands begin to sweat.
The temptation is getting too much,
It calls to me,
'Eat me!' it says.
I want to answer its calls.
My mind says, 'Don't do it.'
But my heart says, 'Go on.'
So . . .
My hands launch forwards,
Off with the wrapper,
In it goes.
Mmmmm, tasty.
It's all silky and smooth.
It's gone.
The taste still lingers both in the air
And in my mouth.
But it soon fades.
Time to find some more I think.

Courtney Newdell (12)
Phoenix School

Untitled

Mouth-watering,
Blood-boiling,
Taste buds annoyed,
　　Let me have it.

Galaxicious,
Gorgeous,
Great,
Galaxy.

I'm pleading, begging,
Just give it here,
The wrapper is just coming off,
It's not me, I swear.

I press it up against my lips,
Closer, closer,
And it's in
Heaven.

Love, I like it,
Chocolatey, eh,
Galaxicious,
I can taste it tingling down my throat.

Now, that's good,
It sends a shiver
Down my spine,
Oh, that's good.

Leah Perry (11)
Phoenix School

Chocolate Room

One day I was told,
If I tidied my room,
I could have one chocolate
From the sexy, lovely, chocolate box.
I cleaned my room,
She went to the shop and got milk!

'Now do the washing up
And you can have another one.'
So I cleaned and cleaned it all up,
So I nicked one and another one
And another hundred!

She saw that they had all gone,
She made me tidy the rest of the house.
I did it all and got £2,
Plus the Celebrations as my favourite:
Maltesers, yum,
Milky Way,
Mars,
Galaxy,
Caramel,
Bounty, yum.

Alex Tarpey (11)
Phoenix School

Untitled

Before I opened the wrapper,
I could only look at it,
It was tempting,
Its creamy looks taunted me,
It shouted, 'Eat me!'

I opened the wrapper,
Hearing the crunchy paper,
Made me think,
As the paper is removed,
The bubbling chocolate is revealed,
Its chocolate looks great,
It's hard to resist.

I wished I could eat it,
There it lay,
On the table,
The creamy wrapper wrapped around it,
I couldn't bear it any longer
And then I grabbed it and ate it.
I could taste the cream,
It felt a dream.

Matthew Russell (11)
Phoenix School

I'm On A Diet

Lick your lips,
Toffee or Twix,
Galaxy Ripple, thin and light,
Chocolate, chocolate, day and night!

The lust, temptation, admiration,
Oh, how I wish I could!
The lovely smooth chocolate,
Slithering down my throat like mud.

Layers of divine flavour,
Make its creamy middle,
The shiny wrapper, I begin to untwiddle.
It hypnotises me, lying there quiet,
Mmmmm, *gone!*
I shouldn't have really eaten it, I'm on a diet!

Emma Childs (13)
Phoenix School

Chocolate

There's a creamy chocolate sitting on the desk,
Shall I pick it up, shall I eat it or guess?
It's tempting me more and more to eat it,
What should I do?
Shall I eat it and follow its rule?
It's dreamy and creamy sitting there,
I can't help but stare.
The smell drifts over my desk,
Tempting me more and more . . .
    Bite!
It tastes so nice!

David Rodrigues (11)
Phoenix School

Food!

Chewy chips, chop, crunchy chips
Crunch, crazy chips
Balmy burgers, batty burgers,
Berserk burgers, bopping on my plate,
Bop, bop, bop!

Jazzy, joyful, jittering jelly
That's just jumped
Out my dish!
Ice-cold ice cream
That's not too old
And not too green.

Ice-cold ice cream
Has just been sold
And tastes like a dream!
Creamy chocolate, charming,
Chocolate, crunching in my mouth!
Charming, crunchy,
Yummm!

Rebecca Mottershaw (12)
Phoenix School

The Sun

Sun, sun, hot sun,
Yellow, orange or red.
Bright sun, shiny sun beams
Down on my head. The sun is
Like a round, yellow lolly shining
All day, especially in April and May.
People love the sun when it shines
And warms them up. At about
Seven o'clock the sun goes
In and I rest my head
For another day
Of sun.

Sally Pugh (11)
Sundorne School

My Motorbike

My motorbike is green,
It makes my mother scream,
My mother sits down,
While I mess around,
This sport is not very clean.

My motorbike is fast,
I hope I don't come last,
The fast rider is called Ron,
My mother shouts, 'Come on,'
It's always the big bikes that speed past.

My motorbike is 85cc,
I ask my friends to come and watch me,
Most say, 'I'm not allowed,
I might get lost in the large crowd.'
Some even get down on their knee.

My motorbike is fantastic,
Some riders are just erratic,
Faster riders are called experts,
When people crash, marshals make diverts,
A man crashed and his girlfriend was dramatic!

Gareth Price (11)
Sundorne School

Green

Green is green, yellow and blue.
Green is green, the colour for you.
Green is green, the grass and the sea.
Green is green, the colour for me.
Green is green, yellow is yellow, blue is blue
And you are you.
Green is green, grass is grass,
The sea is the sea and me is me.

Cerys Pardy (11)
Sundorne School

Summer Days

Summer days
Summer days
Everybody likes summer days.

Where the winds don't blow
And everybody is slow.

Summer days
Summer days
Everybody likes summer days.

When it does not rain
And it does not snow.

Summer days
Summer days
Everybody likes summer days.

Daniel Lloyd (11)
Sundorne School

Football

F antastic teams play in the
O lympics.
O ldham Athletic
T op of the league.
B ottom of the league
A rsenal are the gooners.
L iverpool are The Cop
L eeds got relegated.

C helsea have got the most money.
R onaldo plays with Owen at Real Madrid.
A ston Villa are the best West Midlands team.
Z idane plays with Beckham at Real Madrid.
Y outh teams.

Jack Price (11)
Sundorne School

Autumn

Wind whistling through the trees,
Bare branches everywhere,
Blowy weather whizzing past,
Messing up your hair.

Spooky witches, ghoulish ghosts,
Pumpkins filled with light,
Trick or treaters coming round,
Hallowe'en will give you a fright.

The drumming of the rain at night,
The grey skies in the day,
With it getting dark so soon,
There's not much time to play.

It's raining out there, just out of that door,
Drip-drop, pitter-patter,
There's a puddle just over there,
I'll go and make it splatter.

Kelly Tipton (11)
Sundorne School

Guts

In the Roman days there was no NHS,
So doctors didn't mind if they made a mess.
They found it exciting just playing about,
Getting in your innards and pulling things out.
It was all very new, not done before,
Ripping and tearing the guts on the floor.
People queued outside the door,
Tried and tried to ignore,
And there it was, the gut on the floor,
Smelling of fish, not Lenor.

Scott Mammone (11)
Sundorne School

Autumn

You notice when the leaves start turning
Orange, yellow and gold
That once again summer's turning
Into autumn.

You notice when people get out
Their hats, gloves and scarves
That once again summer's turning
Into autumn.

You notice when the weather starts turning
Rainy, misty and wet
That once again summer's turning
Into autumn.

You notice when the leaves start
Going *crunch* under your feet
That once again summer's turning
Into autumn.

You notice when the air starts turning
A damp but fresh smell
That once again summer's turning
Autumn's definitely here.

Bethan Williams (11)
Sundorne School

Panda Bear

Panda white, panda black
Really heavy, not so light
Creeping through the woods at night
Waiting for a tree to climb
Panda bear, panda bear
Poachers make you all so blind
You care for you mama
You care for your dada
But I don't understand
Why you eat bamboo shoots.

Rachel Hanson (11)
Sundorne School

Holiday

Holiday,
It's a holiday,
With so many things to do!
Holiday,
It's a holiday,
Bet you wish that you could be here too!

When the sun is high,
In an azure sky,
We've been waiting for this all the year.
We can laze about,
We can dance and *shout*,
Make the most of the time we're here!

Holiday, holiday,
Everyone loves a holiday,
Yeah!
Bet you wish that you could be here too.

Andrew Jackson (11)
Sundorne School

Playground

P laying with my friends,
L ong morning before we get there,
A ctivities to do and play,
Y elling and screaming with my friend,
G iggling and crying with laughter,
R unning and screeching after friends,
O pening and shutting doors, rushing to get out,
U nderstanding what my mates say,
N attering to all my mates,
D ay is over and we can play until the day is up.

Emma Davis (12)
Sundorne School

Autumn

Autumn is a colourful time,
It's orange, yellow and brown.
You might need to wear a coat,
Or you could catch a cold!

Autumn is a smelly time,
It smells of bonfires.
It smells of the damp leaves,
That have fallen off the trees.

Autumn is a bare time,
The trees have no leaves.
It is also quite a cold time,
So you may have to wrap up warm.

The crunching and the crispy noises,
The snapping of the twigs,
The whistle of the wind
And the drumming of the rain.

Daniel Francis (11)
Sundorne School

Tigers

They are cunning and can run fast.
They are sneaky and hate water.
The tiger never comes last.
They are stripy and lively.
They are huge and have big paws.
The tiger never comes last.
Tigers, tigers everywhere,
Now I have nowhere to glare.

Timothy Gulliver (11)
Sundorne School

Friends

Friends are brill,
To always just chill,
But they will always be there,
To give you a scare,
But there is a good, a really good side,
They will help you when you slip and slide
And play games like polo or How Low,
Or just talk at the bow.
But friends are not all about games and fun,
They make you feel happy when you are glum.
It's not mean, it's for caring for others,
Like friends, brothers and mothers.
If I lost a friend,
I would go round the bend,
Because friends are special to me
And will always be.

Amy Good (11)
Sundorne School

Playtime

Playtime's good, playtime's bad,
I get my tuck out of my bag.
I talk to my friends,
We play a game,
My friend falls over and grazes her knees.

Playtime's good, playtime's bad,
Especially when you're feeling mad.
I throw my bag, I throw my coat,
I sit down and cry.
Playtime's good, playtime's bad.

Erin Steen (11)
Sundorne School

Tiger's Prey

The prowling tiger
Hunts his prey
What will tiger
Find today?

He spots a deer
To the right
Looks like he's found
His meal tonight.

He tiptoes closer
Not making a sound
The deer's still deaf
Tiger's ready to pound.

His front right paw
Lifts an inch
He arches his back
The deer does not flinch.

He flies in the air
The deer turns
Tiger's claws dig in
Deer's body overturns.

Melissa McIntyre (11)
Sundorne School

There Is Death

There is death,
There is life,
For one to exist,
There must be the other,
For all is life
And all is death,
The time is now
And now is the time.

Stephen Lilico (11)
Sundorne School

Stuff
(Inspired by 'Stuff' by Adrian Michell)

Children sit by it,
People die from it,
Fire!
I hate that stuff.

People eat off them,
Children wash them,
Plates!
I hate that stuff.

People cut themselves on it,
Windows are made from it,
Glass!
I hate that stuff.

People wash with it,
People swim in it,
Water!
I hate that stuff.

Children hate this veg,
Also dogs like this veg,
Sprouts!
I hate this stuff!

Neil Guy (11)
Sundorne School

Dolphins

D ive with grace
O vertake any fish
L ined with silk
P retty as any flower
H igh in spirit
I nteresting to watch
N early all gone
S ave them or pay the price!

Hannah McGonagle (11)
Sundorne School

Teachers!

Mrs Herries
Loves her berries.
Miss Cox
Likes to pick up rocks.
Mrs Ball
Always goes to the mall.
Mrs Garratt
Loves going to Barratts.
Mrs Worrall
Called her child Laurel.
Mr Nance
Never has a chance.
Mr Perks
Eats fizzy jerks.

All the teachers
Are different types of creatures.

Holly Pardoe (11)
Sundorne School

Fish

Fish are funny
Fish are bubbly
Fish are all around me
Fish come up and blow bubbles
Fish are big and small
Fish are fat
Fish are thin
Fish play
Fish sleep
Fish eat
Fish are scaly
Fish are the best.

Katie Griffiths (11)
Sundorne School

Autumn

Walking through the whistling breeze
The cold, wet weather makes me sneeze
Leaves are orange
Trees are bare
Autumn is here, everywhere.

The smell of a bonfire
The screech of a tyre
Icy roads, slippy
We must take care
Autumn is here, everywhere.

The sound of snapping sticks
My watch on my wrist ticks
The skies are black
My woollen hair
Autumn is here, everywhere.

The fires are burning
The clocks are turning
Coats, hats and gloves
The fireworks flare
Autumn is here, everywhere.

Corinne Jones (12)
Sundorne School

Tigers

Tiger bares her yellow teeth
Waiting for her prey
She sees a sloth bear
She gets into position
She pounces with her giant paws
It's true what they say
Tigers are built for the kill.

Steven Lewis (11)
Sundorne School

Autumn

Children dressed up from their heads to their toes,
Their mothers warn them, 'Don't get a bunged up nose.'
Magnificent colours like red, brown and gold,
Many lakes frozen due to the cold.

Crispy leaves to kick around,
The damp, musty smell traps dew on the ground.
Grandmas and grandpas take walks in the park,
Evaporated breaths till way after dark.

A quilt of chestnuts lay thick on the grass,
Robin's eyes watching, as cuddling couples pass.
The fresh, cold air is warmed by the sun,
A fantastic autumn, for everyone!

Lauren Hosking (12)
Sundorne School

PlayStation

P lay games on it
L oad games on it
A ny PlayStation 2 game works on it
Y ou can watch DVDs on it
S o much fun
T he games are good
A ndrew has one
T om has one
I t's really cool
O nce you turn it on, you don't want to turn it off
N obody hates it
2 0 games I have for it.

Daniel Howells (11)
Sundorne School

Autumn

Leaves crunching in the fog
Branches snapping in the cold
Bare trees moaning in the rain
Squirrels chasing nuts.

Fresh air everywhere
Dull blue skies
Dead leaves everywhere but on trees
Creatures hiding for warmth.

Icy roads and people slipping
Scarves, coats, gloves found in all places
As night comes, all loud noises appear
Bang, boom, crash, is only to be heard.

Joshua Steer (11)
Sundorne School

Autumn

Autumn leaves flapping around
Autumn coats can be found
The weather is cold, windy too
All the cows are saying *moo.*

I hear crunching of the leaves
I hear the buzzing of the bees
I hear the snapping of the twigs
I hear the oinking of the pigs.

I smell the night fresh air
I smell the damp without care
I wear my hat, gloves and coat
I wear my scarf on the boat.

Demi Roberts (11)
Sundorne School

Florida!

Florida is hot,
England is not.

The people are nice,
When they eat ice.

They squeal and scream,
It's a Disney World dream.

The Beach Boys were at Epcot,
A very good view I got.

I saw a movie being made,
Then I saw the parade.

Here's my cab,
My holiday was fab!

Abigail Groome
Sundorne School

A Rainy Day

It's a rainy day,
It's time to play,
We love the rain,
When it comes.

Every time it rains,
It's such a pain
When you are not allowed
In the rain.

When it rains
It causes a flood
And when it floods
It is such a pain.

Daniel Briscoe (11)
Sundorne School

A Football Player

A football player
Is trained hard.
He gets tackles in
And he gets in the kicks.
He can run with it.
He can throw it long
And kick it hard.
A football player
Is really good.

A goalkeeper
Is trained hard too.
He kicks it hard
And throws it long.
He can almost hit
The start line.
He can save it
Better than anyone.
He dives better than everyone.
This keeper is the best in the world.

Ben Roberts (12)
Sundorne School

Autumn

Orange leaves flying in the air,
It's cold and it's not fair.
People snapping twigs,
Those little pigs.

It's Bonfire Night,
A little boy is flying a kite.
All we can hear is banging fireworks in the air,
Rockets, Catherine wheels whizzing round my hair.

Lisa Gibson (11)
Sundorne School

Autumn Poem

The whistling winds
Blow the leaves
Wildly around.

Snuffles surreptitiously
Go everywhere to
Infect things.

Brown, bronze and gold
Leaves crunch for
The winter trees.

Fireworks whistle
In my backyard
While chestnuts
Cover the floor.

Foggy mist covers
The bare street
While crispy leaves
Smell.

The twigs of
The bare trees
Snap beneath my
Feet.

Scott Hopkinson (11)
Sundorne School

Autumn

A utumn's coming, leaves are falling
U nder an umbrella you can hear tap, tap, tap
T rees are drumming in the foggy weather
U nder the trees you hear whistling
M um's wearing a yellow scarf
N ever ever go by a smoky fire.

Zoe Charles (11)
Sundorne School

Autumn's Coming

Wind whistling,
Rain pouring,
Autumn's coming,
I can tell.

Leaves falling,
Branches are bare,
Autumn's coming,
I can tell.

Bonfires burning,
Smoky smells,
Autumn's coming,
I can tell.

Bang, crackle,
Fireworks flying,
Autumn's coming,
I can tell.

Cold air,
Damp floor,
Autumn's coming,
I can tell.

Oranges and yellows,
Golds and green,
Autumn's coming,
I can tell.

Naomi White (11)
Sundorne School

The Sponsored Walk

The sponsored walk is waiting,
My brain is debating
What to do.

We've cracked the first mile,
I've walked to the Nile!
How much further?

The second mile is waiting,
My ankle's already aching,
Oh no!

Suddenly the third mile,
I have walked in style
Great.

Halfway there, but then the fourth mile . . .

Yes, it's the fourth mile
I've been alone for a while
Where are my friends?

The fifth mile is waiting
The squirrel is mating
With his new friend.

The final mile at last
I've done this walk quite fast
Whooppeee!

My house is very near
But I've got to make it clear
I've enjoyed it!

Josh Evans (11)
Sundorne School

Animals Galore

Lizards, lizards,
They're not alike,
They run off like blizzards,
That's what I like.

Monkey, monkey,
They swing round like loonies,
They're not very funky,
Just like Wayne Rooney!

Rhinos, rhinos,
They get in rages,
Their skin's like lino,
They shouldn't be put in cages.

Lioness, lioness,
You're so pretty,
Like a princess,
Just like a giant kitty.

Cats, cats,
They eat mice,
They sleep on mats
And are fluffy and nice.

Meerkat, meerkat,
They're nothing to laugh at,
Don't throw spears at,
They're not like any normal cat.

Dogs, dogs,
They rip old tights,
They're a bit like frogs
And sleep through the night.

Stacey Price (11)
Sundorne School

Places

Lovers honeymoon here,
Pizzas are made here,
Italy.
I like that place.

Most things are made here,
Chopsticks are used here,
China.
I like that place.

A very tall tower is here,
Mickey Mouse lives here,
France.
I like that place.

Hamburgers are eaten here,
Big movies are made here,
America.
I like that place.

People love football here,
It is very hot here,
Brazil.
I like that place.

They have big fjords here,
It snows a lot here,
Norway.
I like that place.

They have lots of gods here,
There are lots of poor people here,
India.
I don't like that place.

There are lots of country people here,
Big Ben lives here,
England.
I love that place.

Liam Thomas (12)
Sundorne School

Autumn

The wind whistling in the night,
Twigs snapping when leaves fall,
The drumming rain on the ground,
The noisy fireworks in the air,
Autumn is my favourite season.

The orange, red and yellow leaves,
The bare trees standing alone,
The bare trees are getting cold,
Horse chestnuts drop their conkers,
Autumn is my favourite season.

Autumn is a smelly season,
It smells of leaves and damp,
But on Bonfire Night,
It smells of horrible smoke,
Autumn is my favourite season.

The weather is frosty and wet,
People slip on the ice,
They throw snowballs with the snow,
The air is misty and foggy,
Autumn is my favourite season.

Ryan Davies (11)
Sundorne School

Autumn

A utumn is coming,
U sing woolly hats and gloves,
T rees lose their leaves while raindrops are drumming,
U ltimate breezes hit the air,
M ore and more leaves fall,
N ow I'm inside I can hide.
    I don't have to go back out there.

Robyn Hughes (11)
Sundorne School

Autumn

The whistling of the wind
The dew dampens the lush, green grass
The frost lying there like a white blanket
The icy puddles like diamonds.

The bare trees look at you, sad
All the fiery colours
Red, yellow, orange, the colour of fire
The ground looking like a carpet.

The smell of a bonfire is divine
The smell of leaves is blocked out
The smell of the fire is hypnotic
All around a fine smell.

The conkers waiting to be picked up
Scarves, gloves, a warm feeling
The leaves on the ground,
The sight of a black sky.

The sounds of crispy leaves
The snap of a twig
Bang! Another firework
Splash! Another downpour!

Ryan Owen (11)
Sundorne School

Autumn

A romatic smells of fresh leaves in the morning
U ndercoats and scarves are grabbed on the winter mornings
T all, dead trees are a whitish-brown from the ice
U nder the icy surface of the ground, animals sleep
M ild, windy whistling of the wind whipping through the trees
N oisy fireworks of Bonfire Night go off.

Samuel Rust (11)
Sundorne School

Autumn

Whistling wind, crunching orange leaves
The smell of autumn is in the air.
Wet, frosty morning dew
The singing of birds in the morning.

People with jumpers and scarves
Trying to get past me.
I frown at them but they ignore me,
Smoky smells are in the air today.

The rain tap, taps on me,
I've got a blocked nose.
Umbrella's up, I'm sniffing every day,
While bonfires go on outside.

The weather is windy out there,
I don't want to go out.
But I put my jumper on,
My friends are playing conkers outside.

Ashley Mitchell (11)
Sundorne School

Have You Seen The Sea?

Have you seen the sea, glamorous and beautiful,
Shimmering as it gallops?
Calm as a cucumber, most of the time!
As wide as the solar system,
But also the fury and rage of a lion!
Full of deep sea creatures.
Next time you go, have a little look.
The sea, the wonderful sea!

Summer Robertson (11)
Sundorne School

An Autumn Poem

Foggy and moggy
Damp and wet
Birds aren't singing
So I'm in bed

Broken branches
Crushing leaves
Bare trees
And cold knees

Whistling winds
Drumming rain
Snapping twigs
So I'm cold and in pain

Witches are flying on their brooms
Vampires are drinking blood
Skeletons are rising from their tombs
Trick or treat, it's Hallowe'en!

Jamie Roberts (11)
Sundorne School

Man Utd

M arvellous team
A lways winning against teams
N o chance of losing

U nited are the best
T he best team in the world
D ream team

F ar too good for Arsenal!
C helsea have no chance!

Thomas Butler (11)
Sundorne School

I Love Snakes

Snakes, snakes,
They are so slithery and green,
Snakes, snakes,
Poisonous and deadly,
Snakes, snakes,
There are so many kinds.
There are:
Tree snakes
And vipers
And anacondas,
Grass snakes
And water snakes,
Pythons
And corn snakes
And that's
Why I love snakes.

Michael Bufton (12)
Sundorne School

Football

Red card
Yellow card
Nets, goals and posts

Footballs over here, over there
Beckham's the captain and Sven's the host
The crowd were jumping up and down
There were booming noises all around

Offside, free kick, goal scored
Beckham tops off really quick
Wow! Wow! England won
Let's go off and celebrate, Sven's already gone!

Abi Kelly (12)
Sundorne School

The Baby And Me

I am me and you are you,
That's the way it's meant to be.
Me as me and you as you,
We will play peek-a-boo.
As you sit in your cot,
I am doing dot to dot.
You being you and me being me,
I know your favourite animal is a bee.
Just being you and me just being me.

Jodie Brown (11)
Sundorne School

When Autumn Comes

The blue in the sky when autumn comes.
The smell of the fires when autumn comes.
The sound of the birds when autumn comes.
The sight of the fog when autumn comes.

The redness of the leaves when autumn comes.
The effort of cleaning up the leaves when autumn comes.
The deafening fireworks when autumn comes.

Karl Davies (11)
Sundorne School

Dogs!

Dogs are great
Dogs are man's best friend
Dogs howl at the moon all night long
I love dogs
I wrote this because I had a dog
Who was lovely, fuzzy, furry, hairy,
All that, called Jake.

Tara Broadhurst (11)
Sundorne School

Autumn

Golden leaves crunching as you walk,
Wind blowing icy cold,
Horse chestnuts falling from the trees.

The smell of bonfires,
Hip hip hooray,
See the whistling fireworks go up, up, away.

Another day, wrap up,
Fresh smell every day,
Snotty noses running.

Misty cold air,
Trees shaking with cold,
Branches falling.

Jade Titley (11)
Sundorne School

Spooky House

Number 13 Broadway Street,
It's the spookiest house around,
No one wants to go there because of the spooky sounds.
There are gravestones sticking out of the long, untidy grass
And scattered around the pavement there's lots of broken glass.
You step inside the house and it's even spookier still,
There is a sort of screaming sound, like an electric drill.
I start my long walk home, I hear the thunder crash,
I look up in the sky and see a massive flash.

Kate Marshall (12)
Thomas Telford School

The Awakening Animal

Shiny red steel flashing through the trees,
Like a red-hot flame burning dry wood,
Hugging the tight curves on the road ahead,
Like a newborn baby seeking its mum.

On a clear, flat track, the engine purrs,
Like a contented, sleeping cat,
But as the steep hills rise,
The noise increases to a roaring tiger.

Determined as an athlete to reach the finish line,
The car races on to its final destination,
Speeding along, no thought what's behind,
Like a hungry cheetah hunting its prey.

Suddenly, without warning, it screeches to a halt,
Tyres burning and screaming for mercy,
The car enters a dark, mysterious black hole,
At last the predator returns home.

Daniel Codling (13)
Thomas Telford School

Weather

As the *rainbow* saw me, he signaled to his friend, the *sun*
Who warned me about her brother, the *wind,*
That was throwing big gusts around my body and shouting
                                                    at the *rain,*
And he started shooting down great bullets of water and ice!
As all the weather fought, the *rainbow* slowly flashing her
                                            beautiful colours
Which illuminated the great fight and slowly, very slowly,
The weather stopped fighting and gazed in awe at the *rainbow's*
                                                    beautiful clothes!

Louise Kealy (11)
Thomas Telford School

A Storm

The lightning flashed like a torch,
The wind howled like a wolf,
The thunder shook the ground like an earthquake,
The rain hammered down like hail,

We're in a storm.

The storm is out to get me like a lion.

I feel so cold, like a polar bear,
I feel so scared, like an ant.

I see a blur, like I have vision problems,
I see a flash of colour, like I'm in a rainbow,
I hear the rain, like bombshells,
I hear the thunder, like an elephant.

Someone, help me, please!

Ashley Wilkes (11)
Thomas Telford School

Empty!

A heart without a beat,
Empty

A child without a smile,
Empty

A grave without a stone,
Empty

An adult without a child,
Empty

Me without you,
Empty.

Charley Williams (12)
Thomas Telford School

Bonfire Night

Bonfire Night comes once a year
So I get happy when it's near.
Can't wait to hear the crashes and bangs
And the lovely smell of the hot dog vans.

Where all the people gather around
To see the sights and hear the sounds,
The rockets flying so very high,
Before exploding in the sky.

Holding sparklers one by one
And having fun until they've gone,
Children gazing at the sight,
As fireworks go *bang* through the night.

The guy is burning on the fire,
But soon is gone when the flames get higher.
All the oranges, golds and reds,
Dazzling the children's sleepy heads.

The finale comes when all the fireworks have blown
And everyone's sadly got to go home.
Back through the muddy fields we tread
And all of us are off to bed.

Joseph Cox (11)
Thomas Telford School

Autumn

Red, orange and brown are the colours I see,
As the leaves swirl around the villages and streets,
The days will be shorter, so dull and grey,
As the wind blows colder and stronger each day.

The trees look so lonely and completely bare
And most of the animals have fled elsewhere.
Flowers that once blossomed are here no more,
As autumn returns with the winds that *roarrrrr*.

Amraj Reehal (11)
Thomas Telford School

Lady Autumn

Slowly, she crept in, stealing the throne,
She delicately paints the leaves in tones of golden brown
And sprinkles her frost across the ground.
The memories of summer begin to fade,
As day by day she replaces the warmth with her cool breath.
She brings in the blackness of night and a blanket of stars,
Preparing the streets for a show to her delight.
In the sharp, crisp air, she watches the children with
Glowing pumpkin lanterns, celebrating the ghostly antics of
                                            Hallowe'en.
She whispers to the trees which rustle in her breath,
Waiting anxiously for the next festival - Bonfire Night.
The night arrives with colours and sparkles, crackles and booms.
The explosions illuminate the sky.
Over her shoulder, winter is waiting with an icy stare
And with one last glimpse at her kingdom,
She disappears for another year.

Matthew Poole (12)
Thomas Telford School

Fear

I lay inside my bed one night,
Terrified of the sound of the roaring thunder.

I could hear the sound of the rain,
Hammering down to the ground like a bear stamping his feet.

I could see the brightness of the moon,
Shimmering in the sky like a piece of foil.

I could taste the bitterness of the outside sky,
Creeping past my bedroom window.

I could feel my heart racing as fast as a cheetah,
As I lay inside my bed that night.

Lara Vail (11)
Thomas Telford School

Betrayal Vs Happiness

The colour of *betrayal* is black, like the colour of a hearse.
The colour of *happiness* is red, like the colour of my favourite
                                            football team.
Betrayal is like the world is coming to an end, a series of
                                            catastrophic events.
Happiness looks like children receiving a letter from Thomas Telford
Saying that they have secured a place at the school.
The sound of *betrayal* is a dripping tap with only me close by.
The sound of *happiness* is adults screaming with excitement
As though they have won the lottery.
Betrayal smells of nothing, everything around me is plain,
My scent has died away.
Whilst *happiness* smells of victory, like Liverpool have won the
                                            Premiership.
The taste of mouldy cheese represents *betrayal*.
The taste of the sweetest ice cream symbolises *happiness*.
Betrayal feels like poison circling in my veins and arteries
That rips me into excruciating pain,
And *happiness* feels smooth, like skin,
Because I am alive and I'm proud to live and you should be too!

Rhys Simmonds (11)
Thomas Telford School

Disaster

A strong wind brewed like an old man making beer.
The tornado screamed, defying the Earth.
The lightning ripped down, toasting a tree as easily as
                                            scissors cutting paper.
People ran for cover like terrified ants being squashed by a shoe.
The tornado was back again, blowing things up into its core.
The tornado was destroying, destroying, destroying . . .

Tom Yeo (11)
Thomas Telford School

My Poem

As you step into the doorway,
And hear the creaks above,
Silently and quietly,
You'll hear the whisperers talk.
Scared and frightened,
You take a step more,
Until you see the shattered windows,
They're not asleep anymore.
Shivering and dithering,
Scared to the bone,
You hear a noise beside you,
Then you run through a door.
Now you're in a chamber,
There's no way out,
There's no help around you,
You're shaking like a leaf.

Grace Lamsdale (12)
Thomas Telford School

My Special Garden

My special garden
Hidden through the hedge
Exotic, but yet English
A gardener once said:

'If you care for your garden well
And lock the garden gate,
Your garden will forever grow,
Do it for the flowers' sake
And it will become your own'.

My special garden
Golden, red and green
Flowers come from orange to pink
Make it a pride to be seen.

Natasha Martin-Shaw (11)
Thomas Telford School

Autumn Is . . .

Autumn is a breathtaking thing
The crispy, crinkly leaves are fluttering down
With the tall oak tree, sitting in the park
Children gathering their conkers
To play their inherited game

Pumpkins are being harvested
For the cold, chilling night of Hallowe'en!
It is like evil walking amongst the Earth again
In costumes of gruesome figures

The early mornings will eat you into the cold
Sparkling dew on your front lawn
The fog blocking your sight
With the wind whispering to you
It is autumn . . . it is autumn . . .

Mitchell Norman (12)
Thomas Telford School

My Alien Poem

I met an alien called Flibba,
Who had a brother called Jibba.
They both had green eyes
And heads shaped like pies,
And both smelt of smelly old kippers!

They walked with a trail of slime
And the slime was the colour of grime.
They had four arms
And were fascinated with farms.
I have never seen an alien of their kind.

They had to go home,
Dribbling yellow, frothy foam.
I miss them so much,
With their green, slimy touch,
I'm like a dog without its bone.

Rebecca Cooper (12)
Thomas Telford School

A Martian's Review Of Earth

Beam me down so I can see,
Life on Earth in all its glee.

What strange beings, two ears, two eyes,
The little person who screams and cries.

What a hectic life, no time for pleasure,
No time for their children, no memories to treasure.

The countryside they take for granted,
No appreciation of what God has planted.

Their young grow old before their eyes,
Before they know it, they're saying goodbye.

What is all this fighting for?
Little excuse is needed for war.

Life on Earth will soon be no more,
Because man will destroy himself, that's for sure.

Take me back to my place of birth,
Where I can sit and pray for Earth.

Jamie Mackenzie (12)
Thomas Telford School

An Autumn Poem

Trees change their coats of green,
Autumn's golds and reds can now be seen.
Leaves fall off the trees,
In the autumn breeze.
Acorns fall from the mighty oak,
Garden bonfires give off thick smoke.
Conker shells are ever so prickly,
Children hunt for them really quickly.
Families gather around the bonfire,
Firework rockets go higher and higher.

Harry Lewis (11)
Thomas Telford School

The Little Star

Twinkle, twinkle, little star,
How I wonder how you are.
Up above in the lonely sky,
Like a diamond up so high!

When the hot sun has gone down,
When nothing shines upon the town,
This is when you shine your light,
Twinkle, twinkle, all the night!

In the dark you sit all night,
Always showing your little light.
For you never ever shut your eye,
Until the sun is in the sky!

Little star, don't go away,
Until we see the break of day.
Twinkle, twinkle, little star,
Now I wonder where you are?

Kirsty Jones (13)
Thomas Telford School

My Autumn Poem

Autumn is here
Winter is near
The leaves are falling off the trees
Children scrunching in the leaves
The colours golden, orange and red
While people still sleep in bed
When day is getting colder
The nights are coming nearer
People wearing duffle coats
And it's too cold to stay on boats.

Autumn's great, autumn's fun
Even though there's not much sun.

Joanna Foster (11)
Thomas Telford School

The Veegee!

The Veegee is a mysterious creature which lives in the land
She looks ever so weird with three gnarled fingers on every hand.

She has twenty-four arms and twenty-four toes
Has ten red, piercing eyes and a bright green nose.

Her head turns colours with every emotion
She is like a witch that conjures up potions.

She is extremely tall and can't fit into her bed
No wonder, as she has five spikes on her head!

Her body is large, big and bulky
Her face is like a rat, sad and sulky.

Nobody likes her for she is very ugly
You can't exactly call her all kind and cuddly.

Guess what she has on the end of her nose?
Shall I say, oh I dare not
A bright green, yellow and red gigantic spot.

For this she locks herself away every night
And doesn't come out until noon when it's light.

The Veegee is the freakiest creature I have ever seen
She looks very weird and very mean.

Molly Clarke (12)
Thomas Telford School

Puppy

Puppies are cute, cuddly, curious creatures,
That like to play like mad.
They cuddle you tight in the middle of the night,
When you're cold or feeling sad.

They're fast and friendly and bark is their talk,
They are great company,
Whether sitting, begging
Or on a small walk.

Aoife Kelly (11)
Thomas Telford School

Witches!

Many people live in fear,
That to witches seems quite clear.
With their pointy hats
And witches' brew,
I'd be frightened,
Wouldn't you?

They cast their spells
And make their lotions,
Evil brews and witches' potions.

They make you ill,
They make you bad,
They make you happy,
They make you sad.

Many people live in fear,
That to witches seems quite clear.
With their pointy hats
And witches' brew,
I'd be frightened,
Wouldn't you?

Marie Myler (11)
Thomas Telford School

Autumn

It's here again; autumn has come,
Playing in the leaves, having fun.
A gushing wind, blows trees around,
Whistling and tooting, that frightening sound.
All the leaves are red and gold,
Time to go home, as I was told.
Days get shorter by the hour,
It's time for tea and a shower.
Mum shouts, 'Tom, time for bed,'
Get ready to rest that weary head.

Tom Haynes (11)
Thomas Telford School

The Lotup From Pluto

Everyone heard about it,
It was all over the news,
A strange human being of some kind,
Wandering around in a tomb.

He had six arms and legs,
All in the shade of pink,
Two oval heads, one happy, one gloom,
And his tummy was scarlet-red.

People asked for his name,
He didn't say a word,
He didn't speak a language,
Anyone around here could.

Once or twice he was on TV,
For one thing or another,
He hobbled around from shop to shop,
When people saw they stuttered.

But if they just looked at his skin,
Printed on his arm,
Said, 'Hi, I'm glad to be on Earth,
I'm the Lotup from Pluto.

I don't speak your language,
But I do read your writing,
Write if you want to talk,
Because I'm the Lotup from Pluto'.

Two months on,
And still he wanted to say,
'Hi, what is your name
And where is the nearest space station?'

Emma Sutton (12)
Thomas Telford School

The Slatter From Saturn

There was once a Slatter from Saturn,
Whose body and face were a most peculiar pattern.
I will tell you the story,
I promise it's not gory.

On his face he had six eyes and six ears
And a snotty nose with a mouth and almost a beard.
His teeth were as big as conkers
And could drive him absolutely bonkers.

He had yet again exactly six arms and legs,
He had two fingers on each hand and said he had twelve pegs.
He carried six axes with him and used them to do tricks
And when people passed, they couldn't help but get transfixed.

He was a rather tall and thin young man,
A change from the small, fat people from the Saturn clan.
He always wore a thick, green sash,
That cost a whole bunch of cash.

He had a sister called Daisy,
Who was a little bit crazy.
She was 103 years old
And was always, always cold.

Slatter, the multicoloured fellow,
Was covered in red, blue, yellow,
Green, orange, pink, brown, purple and grey,
He was the sunlight of your day.

Good old Slatter!

Chelsea Norris (12)
Thomas Telford School

The Grumpy Old Man

'Oh, I hate those mobile telephones,
with all that teletexting,
those fancy ringtones,
that pierce your ears
and get on your nerves.
Oh, I hate those mobile telephones!'

'Oh, I hate the kids these days,
no exercise,
no chores,
just playing on their gamestations,
all hours of the day.
Oh, I hate the kids these days.'

'Oh, I hate this new technology,
computers, phones, radios and TVs,
how can anyone keep up?
I know I won't get involved!
Oh, I hate this new technology!'

'Oh, I ha . . .'
'Well,' said his daughter,
'I hate it when you go on like this!'

Matthew Squires (11)
Thomas Telford School

The Spooky House

The houses spied on me as I walked down the street,
The angry wind whistled and whined through the street,
My pace quickened, then I came to a *spooky* house,
The trees waved in the wind, like hands waving to each other,
Then it came up from the ground and said to me,
'Who are you? Who are you? I'll get *you!*'
Then I ran past the trees and the houses to my house,
In my house where it is safe, safe from *it!*

Thomas De Vere (12)
Thomas Telford School

Hurricane Ivan

All eyes on the smoky black sky,
As hurricane Ivan storms his way,
The people of Florida are terrified,
There is no chance that they are going to stay.

Rain pours down on the city streets,
The sky fills with lightning,
Thunder, full volume beats,
The sound of the wind is frightening.

Many homes are rubble and dirt,
Only lucky people did survive,
Thousands of people were hurt,
After the hurricane arrived.

The waves that used to be gentle and kind,
Became big giants,
Ready to blow away your mind,
The waves were not so steady.

Many lives were taken during this disaster,
But now the people return to their homes
And say the hurricane was the master,
But again lies dormant in Earth's bones.

Cassie Lindley (11)
Thomas Telford School

Autumn Is . . .

Autumn is cold and misty,
The hedgehogs are going to bed,
All the slugs and snails leave their trails on the walls
And the leaves are falling from the trees.
They are all brown, orange and red,
The moon is high and bright
And the grass is covered in frost and dew.

Alexandra Burton (11)
Thomas Telford School

Rainbow

Bowing, I see a prism of light,
Of violet, blue and amber bright.

Hovering upon the old horizon,
She reaches for raindrops and grasps the rays,
Like an angel she floats through those long summer days.

The clouds become black,
The rain starts to fall,
Though soon she is gone,
Not left here at all.

Now I can't see the prism of light,
Disappeared in darkness, no colours so bright.

Storms and blizzards whistle and blow,
No longer can we see her luminous glow,
Though here we had seen a beautiful rainbow.

Gemma Wells (11)
Thomas Telford School

Autumn Is . . .

Autumn is the season between sunny summer mornings and cold winter nights.
Autumn is when you know it's nearly Christmas.
Autumn is when golden leaves crash down from ageing trees.

Autumn is when animals start preparing for hibernation.
Autumn is when coats, scarves and gloves start to appear.
Autumn is time for the harvest.

Autumn is when time speeds up.
Autumn is when ghosts and vampires fill the streets.
Autumn's when rockets filled with gunpowder pollute the sky.

Autumn is great!

Daniel Goodall (12)
Thomas Telford School

A Girl

There once was a girl who led a happy life,
Her father used a spanner, her mother was his wife.
They lived at a house in a nice quiet street,
Their dog was brown and had white feet.

Everything was great until a fateful day,
'We're going for a drive,' she heard her mother say.
They were meant to go to a business meeting,
They never had a chance to give a greeting.

Crash went a lorry, *boom* went the car,
It tumbled off a cliff and fell quite far.
The girl was getting rather worried,
Then came a phone call that was rather hurried.

'Hi,' said a voice, 'I regret to inform,
your parents won't see another dawn.'
'They're dead?' she gasped at this phone call,
'Yes, they died in their car, off a cliff they did fall.'

There once was a girl who was all alone,
No father or mother to call her own.
She moved across and just down the street,
With her brown dog who has white feet.

Kelsie Fall (12)
Thomas Telford School

Sadness

Sadness is the colour light blue, like tears,
It looks like a flood of tears washing everything away.
Sadness sounds like a child weeping forever,
It smells like saltwater washing through my brain.
Sadness tastes like a sour sweet upon my mouth,
It feels like a loved one slipping away forever.

Grace Atkinson (11)
Thomas Telford School

Ocean

Ocean, a monstrous, deep blanket
The air sharp as a knife
Seagulls circling like the wheels of a car
Old fishermen sitting dull and bored.

Boats bobbing, swaying on the crystal top
Green as grass seaweed floating, moving in the waves
Tourists eating ice cream, all sticky like treacle
Waves smiting the boats, but gradually calm.

Ice-cold water sending up chilling shivers
Fish gliding through the sea
As they change direction when fish nets come
The sun shining on the gleaming surface.

The waves blinding, crashing down
Like an erupting volcano, powerful and strong
The transparent colour as clear as glass
Ocean, a fantastic yet dangerous place to be.

Louisa Piller (12)
Thomas Telford School

Teenage Sister

Never get a teenage sister
Especially when they're in love
First comes the perfume
Which smells like a sickly sweet flower.

Then there's the make-up
Heavy and full
Like a panda which has just painted
Bright pink all over their cheeks.

Finally there is the ums and ahs
Mum says it's sweet
Then she says something terrible:
'Just wait till you're a teen.'

Bethany Carter (12)
Thomas Telford School

A Thunder Storm Is . . .

A thunderstorm is . . .

A bear's roar
A light bulb going out
The rumbling of my stomach
A fork in a road suddenly illuminated by a street light
A sudden sighting of death
A fire coming towards me at great speed
A cymbal being hit tremendously
God's punishment
My mum glaring at me when I have done something wrong
A sudden rush of energy within the Earth's atmosphere
A pet's hell
A murderer running after an innocent victim
A very welcome friend
Dark
   Lonely
      Scary.

Fraser Grieve (11)
Thomas Telford School

After The Battle!

He stands on the cliff edge, mourning their death,
Cloak flapping in the wind, rippling in the breeze.
He is joined by many, they are with him,
They are at the bottom of the ocean,
They are at the bottom of the sea.
I can see him from my bedroom window,
Just standing, mourning, crying,
But they are there with him, his friends.
The sole survivor, mourning their death,
But they are there with him, his friends.

His ship went down, he survived,
I am grateful, he is guilty,
But they do not blame him - his friends!

Laura Bailey (13)
Thomas Telford School

The Event That Changed The World

As I looked upon those towers,
So magnificent and strong,
The thought never came to me,
They wouldn't last long.

Sadly, many people died,
In this tragic event,
They all thought it an accident,
But it was really meant.

One aeroplane soared across the sky,
The people didn't care,
Until it hit the building
And it went up like a flare.

Not too long later,
Another one did smash
Into the building with such force,
It created a massive crash.

Then the towers fell,
First the south, then the north,
Searching for bin Laden,
We've been back and forth.

They were a brilliant sight,
That became the graveyard of heroes,
For a while they were the tallest,
And now they are Ground Zero.

Thomas Williams (12)
Thomas Telford School

If I Were . . .

If I were a lion, proud to be,
To come and see me, you'd have to pay a fee.
Just imagine what it would be like,
King of the cats and call me Mike!
Next minute you'll be filled with glee!

If I were a giraffe, the tallest ever,
Can anyone be taller than me? *Never!*
I'd be so fragile, that's what I think,
I'd never like to be the colour pink!
Because if I was I'd be loony . . . *forever!*

If I were a snake, slimy and slow,
Once I saw my prey . . . go, go, go!
Get up to gear five, slow, a bit quicker, fast,
Oh no! I lost him. Can't I go back to the past?
If I could, this time I'd catch my foe.

If I were a baby rhino, wallowing in the mud,
Once I'd had practice, I'd soon be good.
Charging through everyone, mighty and fast,
When Daddy comes charging, I just hear a blast.
I can do that. Think I could.

Because I'm me, I know what it's like,
Sporty, academic, riding on my bike,
If I was any one of those,
I'd have a lot of foes,
If I'm a lion, I'd still like to be called Mike!

Jordan Griffiths (11)
Thomas Telford School

A Spooky House

Crash!
The lightning lights up the old, gloomy house,
All alone, nothing there except for the house.
Slowly I begin to open the door,
Its creaking hinges frightening me,
Such a sound I had never heard before.
Cobwebs hang and cling to my face
As I walk forward, one step at a time
Across the old, wooden floorboards.
My heart is beating fast.
I cannot describe how scary it feels.
Not a sound,
The silence seems worse than the noises.

Bang!
Suddenly another clap of thunder,
A flash of lightning and once again, silence.
Silence, as I fall through the air
Floating downwards as the rotten floorboards give way.
Am I dreaming?
Will I wake up?

George Jones (12)
Thomas Telford School

A Snail Is . . .

A swirl of colour
A silky track
A slug with a home
A slimy sack
A silver trail
A blur of slime
A brownish bulk
He takes his time.

Jodie Brown (11)
Thomas Telford School

Planes!

At first sight a plane is like a Pegasus
Galloping in the air,
Two wings spread like eagles
Soaring through the air.
A head like a chimp
Brushing through the air,
A body as streamlined as a seal's.
A tail whipping through the air
As a cheetah's tail whipping through the air
In a race for food.
Wheels running as fast as a lion.
Chairs waiting there ready to be grabbed
Like the control for a TV.
Food coming like a snail running to America.
TVs waiting to be seen and play games on
As if you're in a fun-filled park.

Unnas Nadeem (12)
Thomas Telford School

Autumn Is Here

Leaves are turning red and gold,
Morning air feels chilly and cold.

The darkness quickly comes at night,
Conkers used in the playground to fight.

Hallowe'en goods are in the shops,
It's nearly time to turn back the clocks.

The squirrels are dashing to and fro,
Hiding nuts before the winter snow.

The summer has now drifted away
And it seems that autumn has come to stay.

Emma Murray (11)
Thomas Telford School

Spooky House

As I entered the chamber,
Eyes opened on the walls.
I knew I was in danger.
As I entered the hall,
It was as dark as a cave.
Something rolled out,
It was someone's eyeball.
As I entered the cellar,
Skeletons arose.
I ran back out again and . . .

I ran through the chamber,
The eyes all closed.
I ran through the hall,
The eyeball had disappeared.
I ran through the disintegrating door . . .

I looked back behind me,
There in its place were the ruins.

Was it a dream?
We do not know.

Maddison McNally (11)
Thomas Telford School

A Snail Is . . .

A patterned shell,
A shell of darkness,
An alien from this world.
A spiraling housing estate,
An insect of sturdy armour.
A bird's first choice for tea,
Slower than imaginable.
A slippery, slimy trail of the moon's reflection.

Oliver Woodhouse (11)
Thomas Telford School

Rain

I looked out of the window
Rain!
Another miserable day
Got to stay in I suppose

I looked out of the window
Rain!
Lightning flashed
And thunder rumbled

I looked out of the window
Rain!
What's on TV today?
The same boring EastEnders again

I looked out of the window
Rain!
I think I should do my homework
But first I will have a go on my PlayStation 2!

Mitchell Hill (11)
Thomas Telford School

Colours

Blue is a cloudless sky
Green is the fields that pass by
Orange is a bright, sunny day
White is the mountains far, far away
Red is a flaming fire
Grey is a worn out tyre
Yellow is daffodils blooming
Black is a panther prowling
Pink is a squeaky piglet
Blonde is a tiny girl's ringlets
Purple is a cluster of lavender
Brown is a cheeky chocolate Labrador.

Megan Ward (12)
Thomas Telford School

Having An ERCP (Endoscopy)

Waking up in the morning being found starved,
Waiting to be scheduled on the list,
Getting so excited about going down,
Finding your bed rolling down a hill,
The nurses having a struggle trying to fit the bed in the lift,
Seeing the lift going down three . . . two . . . one . . . ground,
Finally!
Everybody staring at me sitting in my bed,
Standing outside the theatre room,
Being unconscious on the operating table after having the
                              anaesthetic syringed into your cannula,
Hearing yourself count sheep,
Zonked off . . .
Being in 'recovery' wondering what had just happened,
Waiting for my oxygen mask to be taken off
Because of my low breathing after anaesthetic,
Great! Everything is normal,
Back to my old self again.

Kinnery Patel (11)
Thomas Telford School

How I Miss You!

I remember the way you'd speak to me

M ild and kindly, you'd help me see
I n the sad times, times of sorrow
S urely God won't mind if I borrow
S ecrets and jokes, hopes and fears

U nforgettable times, laughter and tears

N ever forget you, that goodnight kiss
A nother thing that I will miss
N an, I miss you!

Louise Pritchard (12)
Thomas Telford School

Ode to Wine Gums

O wine gums you are so wonderful!
My number one,
Your sweet taste and your soft, gummy texture
All your flavours are so brilliant.
Your different shapes, they are so fantastic.
Red or black, yellow or green, you are all individual and special.
My stomach would be empty without you.
O marvellous wine gums.

I will never eat another éclair,
I will never chew another cola bottle.
I will never crunch another Crunchie.
I will never gobble another gobstopper,
I will never touch another toffee,
I will never munch another marshmallow,
I will never look at another lollipop,
I will never swallow another sweet.
Even though you rot my teeth, you are the very best!

Carly-Jade Newnes (11)
Thomas Telford School

Rain

A blanket of water,
As it crashes on the windowpane,
Rain slashes down on the roof,
Like knives falling from the table.

The noise is louder than a machine gun in battle,
It falls from the sky like boulders from a cliff,
You sit inside staring at the rain while it hammers on the ground,
Waiting for it to stop.

Oliver Strothers (11)
Thomas Telford School

Whose Place?

Learning eagerly in a room
Art, English, maybe maths,
Even science, where things boom
This is our place.

A holy building with a steeple
A time to rejoice and talk to God,
Inside there are lots of people
This is our place.

Inside an exciting theme park
People all having fun,
They all say it's such a lark
This is our place.

Nice and cosy all the time
Snuggling up beside a pillow,
Lovely warm feeling, it's divine
This is *my* place!

Laurence Newman (11)
Thomas Telford School

Mum

Mum is nice
Mum is kind
The nicest mums
Are hard to find.

When my mum was 21
She had a nice, skinny bum
And now she's nearly 44
Her bum is hanging on the floor!

Mum is generous
Mum is cool
Mum is keen
Then again, she's sometimes mean!

Jane Driscoll (11)
Thomas Telford School

A Thunderstorm!

A thunderstorm is . . .

An erupting volcano
A quick glance of Hell
A bottle of Coke being opened
My sister in the morning
The brink of destruction
The face of evil
A knife in your heart
A flash of life
A jumping disco
The crowd at a football match
The press when England loses
A unique event
A lovely surprise
A murderer killing a victim
Your worst nightmare about your best friend
A bolt of excitement.

Sean Graham (11)
Thomas Telford School

A Thunderstorm

A thunderstorm is . . .

The anger of God,
A sheet of darkness,
Fireworks coming down from the sky,
Light and dark,
Ying and yang,
A shocking experience,
A world gone dark,
A world dormant of light,
A gunshot from the sky,
The death of many,
A black, never-ending tunnel,
A blinding flash of terror,
A world of black hell.

Dean Richardson (11)
Thomas Telford School

Elm Street

The black stone of the house
Glared at me like a bear ready to pounce.
My shadows cast off the ground.
The wind is whistling and howling like it's speaking to me.
'Don't go in,' it whispers to me.
I open the creaking door anxiously.
I think about my options.
Should I run? I decide.
The wind is violently blowing to try and tire me out.
It was as loud as a skyscraper being demolished.
I stumble once, twice.
I scramble to my feet.
A black figure is stood upright in my path.
'Who are you?' I say.
I think it is a vampire.
He walks into the light.
It is vicar Andrew.
I am saved!

Joshua Whaites (11)
Thomas Telford School

Fear

Then in the distance a figure appears,
A shape distorted by glistening tears,
She's scared and her heart is frozen with fear,
'What's up love?' That's all she wanted to hear.
All she was, was a small, poor little girl,
A tear rolled down her face like a white pearl.
The figure slowly moved up the staircase,
With a big, round, happy smile on their face.
It was her mum come to give her a hug.
They hugged and they looked so snug,
She was happy, but scared, and held her tight,
Her mum made her heart shine with lots of light.

Olivia Walsh (11)
Thomas Telford School

Nature - The Seasons

I walked into the winter's cold,
Trying to be brave and bold.
I was hit by a snowball hard and fast,
Hopefully winter will never last.

Spring has come with the trees so bare,
I can't help but to stand and stare.
They look like claws on a lobster or a crab,
Or maybe a knife ready to stab.

Summer is here, so nice and jolly,
I really wish I had a lolly.
It is hot and I am warm,
I'm so glad that I was born.

Autumn's trees are bright and red,
It's a good job I got out of bed.
I like the colours, I like the shade,
They are as sharp as a cutting blade.

Winter has come, yet again,
It is annoying, like a big red stain!

Steven Copp (11)
Thomas Telford School

Dolphins

A grey or silvery-coloured animal,
A smooth creature,
Cute and friendly,
They glide through the sapphire waters smooth and quick,
Leaping and twirling through the air,
Flipping and crashing as they enter the water again,
A wonderful pleasure to see.

An endangered species.
Look after dolphins, they are gorgeous creatures.

Nicola Martin (11)
Thomas Telford School

Waiting

It's midnight
It's my birthday
I can't wait

I'm wondering what I'll get
Will it be that new bike
Or that new television?

The excitement is building up inside me
I'm going to explode
I can't wait

It's morning
I've thrown my covers off
But when will Mom wake up?

I'm downstairs
Eating my breakfast
I hear footsteps

Yes, she's up!
She's coming
I hear footsteps on the stairs

'Good morning, darling
Happy Birthday
Would you like to open your presents?'

    Yes! Yes! Yes!

Reece Smith (11)
Thomas Telford School

The Sun

The heavens open as the glistening ball knocks at my window,
It is my alarm clock to start the day,
It destroys the night and lifts the dark shadow over the world,
Peace is brought to the Earth as light guides the way of our lives.

Joshua Rogers (11)
Thomas Telford School

The Visitor From Xenog

A visitor came from Xenog,
Floated in the air and said:

'The creatures of this planet
are most peculiar indeed.

They move around in waves
but sometimes in sudden jigs.

They spin around on their heads
and sometimes fall looking dazed.

Lights flash around in all colours,
from bright pink to dark blue.

And sounds of all sorts
boom loudly in this place.

There's one creature at the entrance
who looks big and strong.

Sometimes he lets creatures in
and sometimes he kicks them out.

The most peculiar thing of all though
is that this all happens in the dark.

But when it turns to daylight,
it's as quiet as can be!

Mohammed Qureshi (12)
Thomas Telford School

Happiness

Happiness is an orange colour, that's bright and shiny.
It looks like a heavy, rolling sun.
Happiness sounds like friendship and warmth.
Happiness smells like fresh, warm air, like toast.
It tastes like sweet lemons, that are orange in the sun.
Orange feels smooth, like juice, but hot like lemon pie.

Jessica Tonks (11)
Thomas Telford School

Autumn/Winter

Autumn leaves falling,
Like feathers from the sky,
Leaves changing colours,
Like the traffic lights as we drive by.

The wind blowing hard,
As if it was whispering secrets,
The weather is now changing,
Winter can't be far.

The snow is falling heavily,
Like rocks as it falls,
The snowmen lined up in a row,
Like soldiers lined up for roll call.

The white snow on the ground,
Like a giant white duvet,
The snow starts to melt,
Spring is on the way.

Emma Irwin (11)
Thomas Telford School

The Voice

As I stepped out into the rain,
I heard a voice, through the trees it came.
It knocked on my window and banged on my door,
Spoke to me loudly and threw me on the floor.
It whined and it whistled and told me to move,
Before it started to get in its groove.
I watched and watched as houses were destroyed,
As if they were making it get rather annoyed.

When out in the distance I saw a twister,
Acting in the morning like my sister!
Now I knew where the voice was coming from,
I hid in the shelter until it was gone.

David Pickering (11)
Thomas Telford School

Number 2 Woodlands Road

Number 2 Woodlands Road is often always infested with toads,
But now it's changed for all to see,
It's now infested with ghosts and mummies.
You knock on the door and no one is there,
You knock again and you hear, 'Who's there?'

You walk into the lounge to sit in the chair
And all is just fine,
And then ten mummies walk in,
In a perfectly straight line.
They bring you a drink
And tell you the time.

You run out of the house saying, 'My dinner's on,'
You step out of the door and the house is gone.
No one walks down Woodlands Road anymore,
Because now it isn't infested with toads.

Rebecca Percox (11)
Thomas Telford School

Weather

Closer, closer, closer, floated the murky, shadowy, grey cloud.
Come, come, beautiful, dazzling, glittering, glimmering sunshine.
Look! Here is the beautiful sunshine illuminating the pastel-blue sky.

The wind blew my hair like a hair drier.
Listen, listen, can you hear the trees dancing and swaying?
Look, look, the dewy morning, lime-green grass is bobbing up
                                                      and down.

The sunshine grabbed my spirits and pulled me off the ground.
Drip-drop, drip-drop, here comes the nightmare - *rain!*
Take cover, take cover, everyone lock yourself inside.
The rain kicked down in splinters
And I headed for home.

Rachael Holyhead (11)
Thomas Telford School

Nature

As the butterfly came fluttering by,
Like an eagle gliding through the sky,
The sun smiled in the active day,
Like the flowers following the sun's ray.

Trees are dancing in the night,
Like a boxer having a fight,
It's raining rapidly up above,
Sooner or later the rainbow shows its love.

Squirrels come out onto the lawn,
Like a very silent wisp in the dawn,
Eating food wherever it's found,
Howling and yawning all around.

Fields and fields lay upon each other,
Like a baby and its mother,
Unfortunately, the poem has come to an end,
But still nature is my friend!

Tajinder Poonian (11)
Thomas Telford School

Odd Socks

I've looked in all my cupboards
But they're not hiding there
I've looked under my bed
But there was only a bear.

I think they must be hiding
Perhaps they're with the mayor
Or maybe a big dinosaur
Took them to his lair.

I'm going to be late for school now
And I haven't done my hair
My socks must be somewhere
But I know there's not a pair!

Jessica Haynes (11)
Thomas Telford School

Winter Wind

In the cold and icy winter,
Wind runs like a wild hog,
It pulls at the leaves
And helps to make the fog.

It ratters on the windows
And whistles down the streets,
Then whispers little secrets
To everyone it meets.

It pushes people over
And tugs on scarves and hats,
It also makes loud noises,
That scare the dogs and cats.

But when the winter's over
And summer soon is here,
For all the living creatures,
There's nothing left to fear.

Rachael Kenny (11)
Thomas Telford School

Winter

Winter is like,
A massive frostbite,
The cold wind,
Chills me to the bone.

When the snow falls,
It freezes and
Makes the ground,
As hard as iron.

I wrap up warm,
In hat, gloves and coat,
It makes me feel,
As hot as toast.

Daniel Aston (11)
Thomas Telford School

Winter Bites

Frost came knocking on the door of Town
Howling, 'Let me in, let me in!'
Without waiting for a reply, Frost silently crept into town,
Beginning his week-long invasion.

Right behind Frost came his father, Wind,
Who came tearing down all of the golden leaves,
Scattering them along the pathways,
While Frost covered Town with his long white robes.

Wind, however, moved on from Town,
To Town's younger brother, Village.
He huffed and he puffed at all the people until,
Hurricane arrived, taking over his work.

So now the two brothers belonged to
Frost, Wind and Hurricane.
All they needed now was a bit of Snow,
Until guess what? That too, soon came.

Thomas Collier (11)
Thomas Telford School

Happy Birthday To A Special Friend

Happy birthday to a special friend,
All the happiness to you this precious day!
Part of me knows just what I should say
To a special friend, Lewis Sedgley.
You're the boy who keeps me bright,
Before you there was only he,
But now you have put sense into me,
Without you I wouldn't have light.
To me you are always someone I can tell
My secrets, my feelings, you will keep me at bay.
Even though I wouldn't do crime,
I hope you will always keep me in a straight line.
You are my sun and my shade,
My sweets and my wine!

Connor Goldson (11)
Thomas Telford School

Murder At Midnight

One murky night, when the rain tumbled down,
A burnt body was found on the outskirts of town.
To the gruesome scene, the police who came
Observed splattered blood and dismembered remains.
Their task - to unravel the torturous tale,
Uncover the cause of the crime, without fail!

Could it have been a demented mind
Or simply an accident of some kind?
Who was it who caused such despair?
What was it that made them do it there?
The detectives suspected a frenzied fight,
Had occurred on that misty, murky night.

The police searched the county far and wide,
But nothing was found, however they tried.
Until one Christmas Eve, when they received a call,
From an anonymous witness who had seen all.
The criminals were quickly thrown into jail,
Without any mercy, not even police bail!

Dafydd Francis (12)
Thomas Telford School

War

Dodged the bullet,
Missed the knife,
Scared in the bomb shelter,
I want a new life!
I want peace and harmony,
I don't want to be at war,
I want peace and harmony,
They should pass a new law.
The message that I'm trying to say is:
Don't fight.

Victoria Green (12)
Thomas Telford School

The Football Game

On the football pitch
There's a little titch
Who wants to play a game
We've all said no
That he's got to go
Because he's a real pain

He keeps telling us
'What is all the fuss?
I only want to kick the ball'
We let him have one shot
Where he fell on his bot
My, it was a great big fall

He was covered in mud
So he pulled on his hood
And he left and went back home
We all laughed and said
He shouldn't have got out of bed
But stayed there on his own

We carried on with the game
It was a real big shame
Because we lost one nil
So we all went home
And we had a moan
But really the day was brill.

Nicholas Lane (11)
Thomas Telford School

Indian Truck

My dad owns an Indian truck
And got himself into a ruck
He fell on his bum
Bounced onto his tum
So guess where the spices got stuck?

Curtis Goodman (11)
Thomas Telford School

Winter

Autumn taking over the world,
Leaves, crispy brown,
Building up power every second.

Winter strikes, the battle is on,
For many days it lasts,
Until finally Winter succeeds.

He transforms green grass into spectacular snow,
Spiderwebs into glistening,
Sparkling ice,
And he kills plants and trees as he passes by.

Rumours spread!
'He's like a serial killer!' they say,
'And he's spreading like a deadly virus!'

But alas, his icicle powers are fading,
And he knows his time is coming,
When Spring shall unleash all her might!

Suddenly . . .

Spring attacks,
And Winter's life is fading,
And now at last the nightmare ends.

'But soon!' Winter speaks,
'I shall be back again,
To haunt you for another time!'

Lewis Sedgley (12)
Thomas Telford School

Autumn Is . . .

Leaves falling
Wind calling.

Weather bending
Summer ending.

Chloe Simister (11)
Thomas Telford School

Poor John Journey

Poor John Journey,
If only he'd known,
Maybe the tree wouldn't
Have crushed his bone.

John was getting ready,
To go fishing you see,
In his faithful old car,
To be crushed against the tree.

For he was a member
Of a local fishing club,
In his home town,
That was part of a pub.

Johnny set off,
In his little Cavalier,
Only to become
'Tragedy of the year'.

Up the road he drove,
Speeding with ease,
There was a BMW,
The Z4 series with lots of cc's.

Just touching 70,
Starting to overtake,
There was an oncoming Peugeot,
What a big mistake.

The screeches were heard from a distance away,
Hitting the front of the Z4, pounding his head
And the back of the Peugeot,
Poor Johnny was dead.

It wasn't just poor John Journey that suffered that day,
It was his family too.
A young son called David
And a daughter called Sue.

Poor John Journey,
Why did he hit the tree?
Why travel at such excessive speed?
The coroner's verdict, 'a tragic mystery'.

The moral of this story,
What a terrible, accidental waste
Of a man who wanted to get where he was going and crashed,
So remember, 'more speed, less haste'.

Bobby Standley (12)
Thomas Telford School

The Land Of My Dreams

I see her, and she calls to me.
A voice as delicate as the rose.
Ringing through the mountain valleys,
Of The Land of Dreams.
I know that I must go to her,
She brings me, beckons me softly
As I glide through fields full of dancing poppies
In The Land of Dreams.
I can feel myself getting closer as I enter her empire,
I can see the world standing,
Holding hands in The Land of Dreams.

Yet, as I awake, I do not hear her heavenly voice,
I hear bombs.
Instead of mountain valleys, beautiful and true,
I see bottomless pits of deceit and despair.
And instead of the glorious fields full of poppies,
I see desolate and bleak lands of pain.
And worst of all, I don't see the world holding hands,
I don't see them being joyful together.
I see envy, hatred and war.
This is when I wish I was back,
In The Land of Dreams.

Poppy Bennett (13)
Thomas Telford School

Alien Dance

On landing on the planet Earth,
I spotted a roofed wall,
From inside came a booming noise,
A throbbing, then a call.

I glided inside the primitive building,
The monstrous noise was great,
I think the noise was a type of music,
Which I don't think my people would highly rate.

The bodies inside were jerking spasmodically,
Writhing around the room,
It might have been a tribal dance,
But it was nothing like we do on the moon.

I still don't understand why the females,
Adorn skirts and war paint,
Why there were flashes of light and colours,
Just thinking of the swirling mass, makes me feel very faint.

Charlotte Housden (12)
Thomas Telford School

Sadness

Sadness is a gloomy black cloud that looms over all in mourning,
It appears as a wrinkled woman crying over her dead son.
Sadness sounds like a painful crying that pierces the souls of
                                                        all who feel it.
It smells like a fire that has let out smoke that covers the sun.
Sadness tastes like an enormous cranberry that bursts in your
                                        mouth, spreading its sourness.
It feels like cold, bony fingers crawling down your spine.
For sadness is not death,
But death is sadness.

Jamie Hannah (12)
Thomas Telford School

A Poem About Autumn

I wake up in the morning
And see the gold-red leaves,
I can see the day is dawning
And the birds upon the trees.

I slowly walk outside
And greet the cold autumn air,
I put on a coat and decide
To run without a care.

I can feel the cool wind rushing
And trying to hold me back,
I will just keep on pushing,
Until I start to slack.

But that will never be,
I can feel it in my soul,
I hope it never ends,
To go forever is my goal.

Autumn is the best,
Greatest season ever,
If you put it to the test,
It wouldn't lose, never.

Chloe French (11)
Thomas Telford School

Colours

Blue, blue, blue is the sky,
It changes every moment as it passes you by.
Green, green, green are the trees,
A glimmer of sunlight, in between their leaves.
Red, red, red is a rose,
A sign of love and passion it shows.
Yellow, yellow, yellow is the sand,
Warm and glittering, upon the land!

Gina Tarantonio (12)
Thomas Telford School

I Know This Martian

I know this Martian
He has pink, furry skin,
His eyes are like jelly
And his ears are like fins.

His skin's all lumpy
And his dreadful breath stinks,
He moves like a monster
Bang, clink, clink.

He thinks he looks so scary
Yet he's only two foot tall,
But he's not a monster
Just a pink, furry ball.

I know this Martian
He has pink, furry skin,
He's my new cool mate
Though he can't communicate!

Jesica Beaumont (12)
Thomas Telford School

Knock

The cold and scary twilight,
When the bats fly out,
Beginning of the rainy night,
The spiders crawl about.

The imaginary knock at the door,
As the lights flicker,
There's blood on the floor,
I cry and I pray, but . . .

No one can say,
When morning has dawned,
Who killed the poor girl
For whom they mourned?

Shawnee Blackmore (12)
Thomas Telford School

The Sun

The sun is . . .
    A lion's mane
    A light in an empty room
    The retreat of the dark
    A fire spreading across the world
    Blazing
    A yellow ball bouncing up then down
    Blinding to the naked eye
    The yellow ball stuck in the world above
    A victim of dark
    The kidnapper of dark in the dawn
The sun is . . .
    rising
        staying
            then setting.

Nicola Kerr (11)
Thomas Telford School

The Bat'leth From Planet Zog

The Bat'leth from planet Zog,
Was originally spawned in a steaming bog,
Its inner mouth and horrific talons,
Can rend flesh with hideous malice.

It has an elongated head,
And its spitting acid will make you dead,
Its massive mandibles with razor-sharp hands,
Can crush you into pieces that equal thousands.

You wouldn't want to be invaded by him,
Because you will be enslaved by him,
He will make you mine his minerals
And make you lick his limbs.

Erin Davies (12)
Thomas Telford School

A Martian Sends A Postcard Home

I am a stranger
To this world

And before me,
A place so strange

Tall things,
Small things

Parts of them waving,
Shaking

Booming noises,
Flashing lights

Having fun,
Laughing faces

What is this place
So strange?

Natalie Hope (12)
Thomas Telford School

Winter

The winter is cold
We can't wait until spring,
It makes you shiver
But it doesn't make you sing.

It's dark too early
And you can't see a room,
It's like being locked in a cave
Full of fog and gloom.

Make sure you're wearing layers
It's not at all warm,
Sometimes in the day
But especially at dawn.

Sukhvinder Gill (11)
Thomas Telford School

Autumn Is . . .

Autumn is
Fresh, misty mornings,
Dew-covered spiders' webs sparkling in the sunlight,
Children laughing as they run joyfully through piles of leaves.

Autumn is
A blanket of reds, golds and browns covering the countryside,
Short, cold days and long, cosy nights,
Snuggling up next to the fire with my favourite book.

Autumn is
Conker picking on Sunday afternoons,
Pumpkins glowing in the windows on Hallowe'en,
Toffee apples and sweets for good children.

Autumn is
Crackling bonfires and noisy fireworks illuminating the sky,
Children with rosy cheeks wrapped up in hats and scarves,
Sparklers twinkling in the darkness.

Autumn is . . . fantastic!

Lois Perkins (12)
Thomas Telford School

The Wind

The wind is beastly to people
Like the blow of God
A breeze from another world
From the edge of the world
It comes.

A clear blanket
A blowing storm
Like a blow from the mouth
Comes with most weathers
In all places known.

Matthew Jones (11)
Thomas Telford School

A Vimbo From Venus

I'm a Vimbo from Venus
That's all I have to say
As I was made fun of
Just the other day.

I landed on Earth
And I stood out straight away
With my bright green hair
And with skin the colour grey.

I have five eyes
And twenty fingers and toes
I am seven foot tall
And have a big spot on my nose

I asked a boy
'What is the time?'
He just laughed and said,
'Telling an alien would be a crime!'

I walked and found a woman
'What are humans like?'
She just laughed and said,
'You're having a laugh, on your bike!'

I just sat and said,
'I want to go home,'
But that was impossible,
I was all alone.

I am a Vimbo from Venus
That's all I have to say
As I was made fun of
Just the other day.

Becki White (12)
Thomas Telford School

A Very Special Friend

A magic feeling grips me
The time has almost come
To meet someone very special
A friend who will be fun

I wonder, will he like me?
I really hope he will
We'll be the very best of pals
And I'll look after him if he's ill

The time is getting nearer
My heart is beating quick
Come on, come on, oh please
I'm feeling rather sick

The door begins to open
My dad is standing there
In his arms a blanket
I see a tuft of hair

It's what I've always wanted
I've said my prayers each night
I open up the blanket
And see this wondrous sight

He looks at me, I start to cry
A friend for whom I'll care
Two tiny eyes, a cold, black nose
A mass of golden hair

I've waited oh so long for this
I just have to pick him up
He starts to sniff and licks my face
My very special pup.

Kate Breeze (11)
Thomas Telford School

Untitled

I could be a flower, a stone or a tree
The wind on your face
A wave on the sea

I could be your best friend
Looking so normal
Or I could be a businessman
Dressed up all formal

I can change my shape
My size, my smell
I go undetected, I hide so well

For I am an alien
Not from here
I come from a faraway stratosphere

My job is to watch you
Report on your ways
Tell all to my leaders
Who could invade Earth in days

I could be a flower, a stone or a tree
I could be just anything . . .
You'll never see me!

James McIntyre (13)
Thomas Telford School

All The Sweets On Earth

Had I all the sweets on Earth,
Enwrought with sugar and additives,
The Haribo and Starbursts galore,
Of shops full to burstin'.

I would spread the Earth in all the sweets of the world,
But I being healthy have only a few,
I have my favourites that I love and cherish,
So I won't share them with you.

Amelia Reynolds (13)
Thomas Telford School

Darkness

The sun is hibernating
Sucked up stars, no longer shining
A black panther prowling around
Forever searching for light
A bottle of Coke
A phantom covering the earth below
Darkness
Black on a wasp is darkness, yellow is the sun
The final countdown to death
Nothing to be seen
Horror is waiting
A hole in the sky, a road to death
Never-ending darkness
A place where nightmares live
Loneliness.

Christopher Newbury (11)
Thomas Telford School

A Lightning Storm

A lightning storm . . .
A flash of light frightening and freaky
Yellow fills the sky, you might think you'll die
Can't sleep
Starting to weep
From under your covers
Weird noises
Pouring rain
Feels as though you're in pain
Count to 10; 1, 2, 3, 4, 5, 6, 7, 8, 9, 10
There it goes again
Smash!
Heard it!
Saw it!
Don't want to hear or see any more of it!

Lucy Poole (11)
Thomas Telford School

Bullies

Back to school once again
The children all trudge in,
Knowing that they're going to meet
The bully once again.

He's one foot taller than everyone else
And very much stronger too,
He chooses a victim every day
And makes their day turn blue.

Our teacher can't control him
Nor the headmaster,
He practically rules the school
He's already made the lessons faster!

He loves picking on people
Always making their lives hell,
And he's always listening for
The end of schooltime bell.

Tara Grant (11)
Thomas Telford School

Panther

His eyes like a hawk,
Awaiting its prey,
The bringer of death.

He hunts like a monster,
Teeth as sharp as razors,
Striking his prey like an arrow.

His game is to kill,
The body like black oil,
His angelic body showing no more.

Joshua Reynolds (11)
Thomas Telford School

Autumn

The morning grass is sprinkled with silver icing,
The gold-brown leaves make a carpet as they hit the ground,
The cobwebs glisten like silk,
The morning frost glides across the ground.

The dark clouds roam the skies,
It's like a torrent of darkness,
The sun has vanished from the background,
As the wet weather closes in.

As the trees begin to show nakedness,
The animals gather food for their long rest,
The ground is fresh all through the season,
The colours are delightful to see.

Autumn is an unfinished painting.

Alex Liversage (12)
Thomas Telford School

The Universe

The universe is like a big packet of Revels
Being blown by a straw,
Like miniature planets with differing insides
Being wrapped in plastic.

The universe is like shiny marbles
In a pitch-black cupboard,
Or tennis and ping-pong balls
Orbiting a football.

I think that if the planets in the universe
Were a packet of Revels,
My dust rings on Saturn and Uranus would be fizzy laces
And meteors would be Skittles.

Andrew Stewart (11)
Thomas Telford School

Ode To Kittens

Hail, all kittens,
Cutest creations of all time.
Your fur is so soft and shiny,
As I stroke it gently,
I hear the lovely, low rumble of your wonderful,
Happy purr.
Those tiny little paws, so small and unique,
Go pitter-patter, pitter-patter,
As you run obediently by my side.
I shall never hug another hamster,
Nor cuddle another koala,
Nor stroke another seal,
Nor pet another puppy.
For you, O marvellous kittens, are the greatest creatures
That have ever existed and I could never live my life
Without kittens.

Claire Brown (11)
Thomas Telford School

Pounding Puppies

What are they exactly
Except for barking bananas
And chewing champions?
Eating snow, grass and leaves
All day
And their toys and teddies
Of course.
Biting us all the time
Fluffy, cute and cuddly
They get away with it
Each time.

Emma Tranter (11)
Thomas Telford School

The Television

Its square body fills the corner of the room
Its many heads bob up and down in a colourful whirl
Its jaws snap shut when its belly button is pressed.

Big or small, fat or thin
It will hypnotise the human watching it carefully.
Green, grey, blue or bronze
It will catch the attention of anybody willing

For horror, comedy, sadness or love
It has hundreds of moods
There will be one to suit
Everyone.

It even has clothes - which top will it choose?
Cable, satellite, Freeview or Sky?
Or just a plain jacket
With only five buttons to use.

Jack Collier (11)
Thomas Telford School

What I Am

My life is such a daydream
An adventure every day,

From dawn to dusk I'm rushing
With no laughs or play.

I'm in a dizzy, dopey daydream,
That's what most people say,

A person who is crazy, happy mad,
Which my friends say is OK.

A control freak in the making,
Or a teacher on high pay!

I'm not exactly 'normal',
But I'm just made that way.

Salli-ann Mathews (11)
Thomas Telford School

The Dolphin

Rapid glider
His fins move from side to side
While he cuts through open water.

Ear-ringing chatter
His smooth tongue vibrates
When communicating with near surrounders.

Graceful athlete
His twisting and turning
Amazes close-by viewers.

Charlotte Armstrong (12)
Thomas Telford School

A Bird

A bird . . .
Flies in the sky like a plane,
Swooping down like lightning,
Stopping only to pick up his prey.

He is a satellite circling the world,
Never stopping, only resting,
He's an insect's nightmare
And a bringer of death to all worms.

Joel Hibbert (11)
Thomas Telford School

Snow

A blanket of snow,
A haven of peace,
A forest of whiteness,
A sheep's fleece,
A cold fridge,
A dead land,
A lonely place never to be found!

Jessica Skinner (12)
Thomas Telford School

Autumn Is Here!

It's autumn again, it starts to get cold,
All the leaves are turning different shades of gold.
The trees are looking bare as the leaves start to fall,
But oh, what fun it is to walk and kick them all.
The nights draw in and the clocks turn back,
When we come home from school, it's nearly black.
The early morning dew is autumn's best,
When all the spiderwebs glisten and the hedgehogs start to nest.

Lucy Coles (11)
Thomas Telford School

Autumn

The autumn mist in the air,
The foggy sky which makes me scared,
The grey, wet, cold, frosty mornings,
So boring.

The golden moon in the night,
The Hallowe'en costumes they give me a fright,
The golden, red and brown leaves,
From the old oak tree.

Keesha Carpenter (11)
Thomas Telford School

Autumn Leaves

A lways leaves falling, a carpet on the ground
U nderfoot is orange
T rees are golden-brown
U p in the branches squirrels run around
M aking yellow leaves drop down
N ever-ending leaves.

Robin Allard (11)
Thomas Telford School

A Thunderstorm

A thunderstorm is . . .

A loud, roaring, scare tactic,
A cry for help,
A young child's phobia,
Drizzly and smelly,
A crash when it hits the ground,
A light source at night,
Harry Potter's scar.
A thunderstorm is hearing you breathe deeply.
A thunderstorm is causing an enormous puddle.

Kalpna Ahir (12)
Thomas Telford School

Ode To A Rugby Ball

Oh, rugby ball, you are the best by far
When you are spiralling you shine like a star
When Jonny Wilkinson takes a kick over the post
You go so far, you sail past the coast
When Josh Lewsey kicks you, I have no fear
Because you travel as fast as a catapulted deer
So in the morning when you are eating toast
Just remember who got kicked over the post.

Matthew Pacey (11)
Thomas Telford School

What Is It?

It is like a snowman standing in the snow
Like a ball floating in the swimming pool
A boat sailing across the sea
A fish's nightmare.

My pet duck.

Samuel Deakin (11)
Thomas Telford School

A Martian Sent A Postcard Home

Some creatures came from Moonstar
Landed down and said:

'You creatures go around and around
high in the air, up and down

thrown around on whizzing shells
sounds, movement, pink everywhere

people come from all around
to stop and stare

drinking, eating, laughing
at a wonderful place, never bare.'

Abigail Cooper (12)
Thomas Telford School

Winter Is Here!

Summer has gone,
Winter has come,
The snow has arrived,
Time to have some fun!

Winter is here,
Christmas is near,
Time for Christmas parties
And dads drinking beer!

Gather the family round,
For the Christmas feast,
Lovely Christmas turkey
And after . . . time for treats!

Kerry Lancaster (12)
Thomas Telford School